WHEN PELÉ BROKE OUR HEARTS
Wales and the 1958 World Cup

Mario Risoli

St David's Press

Published in Wales by St David's Press

an imprint of

Ashley Drake Publishing Ltd.
PO Box 733
Cardiff
CF14 2YX
www.ashleydrake.com

First Impression – November 1998
New Edition – October 2001

ISBN 1902719 02 6

British Library Cataloguing-in-Publication Data.
A catalogue of this book is avilable from the British Library.

Typeset by WestKey Ltd., Falmouth, Cornwall.
Printed in Wales by Dinefwr Press, Llandybie, Carmarthenshire.
Cover design by www.darkangeldesign.com

CONTENTS

ACKNOWLEDGEMENTS

I would like to thank Ceri Stennett, the Welsh FA's football historian, who has been so generous with his time and knowledge. Thanks also to David Collins, secretary of the Welsh FA, for allowing me access to the FA's records from the 1958 World Cup, and former Daily Express journalist Jim Hill for his memorable anecdotes from Wales's qualifying matches. I am also grateful to publisher Ashley Drake who recognised this story needed to be told. I must also thank my wife, Catherine, for all her help and support while I was writing this book.

Above all, I want to thank the 17 players I interviewed. They are listed alphabetically: Colin Baker, John Charles, Mel Charles, Trevor Ford, Alan Harrington, Ron Hewitt, Mel Hopkins, Cliff Jones, Ken Jones, Ken Leek, Terry Medwin, Ken Morgans, Des Palmer, Ron Stitfall, Derek Tapscott, Colin Webster and Stuart Williams.

All photographs have been kindly provided by the Western Mail and Echo Limited except where stated.

PREFACE

I bought *When Pelé Broke Our Hearts* after reading a newspaper article about it. At the time there was a glut of new rugby and football books, but no new stories. Mario Risoli's book was different. It seemed intriguing and undiscovered.

I had a 24-hour flight coming up at the beginning of 1999. The band was flying to Australia where we'd been invited to take part in the country's 'Big Day Out' festival. I hate flying and this book seemed like the perfect companion. After a full day and night on the plane, the book was finished and the flight, for once, was bearable.

As a young football fan I remember seeing Pelé's first World Cup goal without quite realising it was against Wales in the quarter-finals of the competition. I came across the goal again while reading a wonderful book about football's great goals, which was full of illustrations, descriptions and photographs. At the age of 12, it dawned on me that Wales once had a truly great football team.

My father spoke of the Welsh players who featured in the 1958 World Cup – men like John Charles, Cliff Jones, Ivor Allchurch and Jack Kelsey – as giants, both physically and mythically. Because of this book, which tells the complete story of that campaign, the seed sown in my head as a child has now been fully realised.

Their exploits of that team are all the more remarkable when you consider the amateur set-up that existed at the time – lost kits, missed planes, no singing on the bus, except for hymns. It adds up to a fascinating tale, and it's beautifully told in *When Pelé Broke Our Hearts*.

So enjoy the story of our country's greatest ever football performance and salute the players who, despite being surrounded by chaos, performed so brilliantly.

Nicky Wire, Manic Street Preachers

FOREWORD

IN my opinion, the late Fifties was the golden age of football and the 1958 World Cup remains one of the finest tournaments of all time. There were some great teams in that competition – France, Sweden, West Germany and, of course, the winners, Brazil.

Some terrific players starred in this World Cup. A number of the Brazilians spring to mind. Pelé, who scored the goal that beat Wales in the quarter-final, became an international star in Sweden. Then there was midfielder Didi, who made Brazil tick, and Garrincha, one of the greatest wingers the world has seen.

France also had some great forwards, namely Raymond Kopa and Just Fontaine. Fontaine finished top scorer with a record 13 goals. Sweden, the hosts, were a great team in 1958 with Liedholm, Hamrin and Skoglund. I knew all three well since they were playing in Italy when I joined Juventus. West Germany had Fritz Walter and Uwe Seeler while England boasted Billy Wright and Tom Finney.

As for Wales, we were a good side rather than a great one. Some think it was the best team Wales has ever had. I don't agree. It was one of the best, but not the best. We had comradeship and a wonderful team spirit and that was what got us through. I must also mention our manager in 1958, the late Jimmy Murphy. All the players thought the world of him. Jimmy was the best motivator I've ever come across. He was serious when he wanted to be, but he could also relax with the players and have a drink with us.

Looking back at the team of '58, Jack Kelsey, our goalkeeper, was a good stopper. In defence was Mel Hopkins, one of the best full-backs in British football, my brother Mel who was voted best centre-half of the World Cup, Dave Bowen, the captain and a tireless worker, and Stuart Williams and Derrick Sullivan, who were both very underrated players. The inside-forwards were Ron Hewitt and Ivor Allchurch. Ron was a very good player on his day while Ivor was world-class. He could do anything – score, beat opponents and help out the defence.

We also had two excellent wingers. Cliff Jones was very quick. He would bore down the line and cross the ball. Terry Medwin was different. He would try and beat his man. Together they made a good combination.

As for myself, I didn't have a great World Cup, just a decent one. I had some good matches and a couple of bad ones as well. I was a marked man and the Hungarians kicked me to pieces in the two matches we played against them. I also missed the Brazil game through injury and this remains the biggest disappointment of my career. Still, my memories of Sweden are happy ones.

All four British teams qualified for Sweden and the fact Wales were the most successful was very satisfying, especially since no-one, not even the Welsh selectors who booked their flight back after the last first-round match, gave us a chance. England and Scotland were eliminated in the first-round and even though Northern Ireland joined us in the quarter-finals, their 4–0 defeat by France took some of the shine off their performance. Wales, on the other hand, stunned the world by holding the mighty Brazilians for 73 minutes.

Sadly, not many people know of our achievements in the 1958 World Cup so I'm delighted a book has finally been written. It's long overdue.

John Charles, October 1998

CHAPTER ONE

CHRISTMAS COMES EARLY

DECEMBER 15, 1957. At the headquarters of the Federation Internationale de Football (FIFA), which overlooked Lake Zürich, a draw was made to decide which nation would play Israel for a place in the 1958 World Cup in Sweden.

Israel had qualified from the Asia-Africa section, but by default. Because of the volatile political situation in the Middle East, the Arab nations – Turkey, Indonesia, Egypt and Sudan – had all refused to play Israel. This meant the Israelis topped their group without having to play a single match.

However, FIFA decided that no team could take part in the World Cup, apart from the hosts and the holders, without playing some sort of qualifying match. It came up with an ingenious solution. Israel would play one of the second-placed teams from the European section. Into the hat – the ornate, gold Jules Rimet Trophy – went Wales, the Republic of Ireland, Holland, Bulgaria, Poland, Romania and the runner-up from the still unfinished Group Eight, which would be either Italy or Northern Ireland. One of these countries would be granted a dramatic World Cup reprieve since only group champions qualified for Sweden.

The team that was picked to face Israel was Wales. For the team's manager, Jimmy Murphy, the players, and above all the poverty-stricken Welsh FA, Christmas had come early. Ten days early, to be precise.

Wales's bid to reach their first ever World Cup began in Cardiff, 13 months before Sweden and Mexico kicked-off the 1958 competition in Stockholm. Wales were drawn in European zone Group Four and their two rivals both came from behind the Iron Curtain, Czechoslovakia and East Germany. It was a tough group, far tougher than England's, who had Ireland and Denmark to deal with, and arguably Scotland's as well, the Scots having to do battle with Spain and Switzerland. Out of the four home countries

Northern Ireland, drawn with Italy and Portugal, had the most difficult group.

Wales's first qualifying match was against the powerful Czechs at Ninian Park, on May 1, 1957. In the days leading up to this match Murphy received both good and bad news. The good news was that Juventus, the club star forward John Charles had just signed for, would release Charles for the Czech match. The bad news was that Swansea Town's supremely gifted inside-left, Ivor Allchurch, was injured. Furthermore, left-back Mel Hopkins and outside-right Terry Medwin, the two Tottenham players, would arrive in Cardiff just 24 hours before the kick-off because Tottenham insisted they play in what was an unimportant league match against Burnley.

For the vital opener Murphy, who was assistant manager at Manchester United, named the following team: Kelsey (Arsenal), Stitfall (Cardiff City), Hopkins (Tottenham) Mel Charles (Swansea Town), John Charles (Juventus), Bowen (Arsenal), Medwin (Tottenham), Tapscott (Arsenal), Webster (Manchester United), Vernon (Blackburn), Jones (Swansea Town).

For Colin Webster, a forward on the fringes of the outstanding-United first-team at Old Trafford and who Murphy described as "a formidable opportunist", it was his first Welsh cap. Vernon replaced Allchurch while John Charles would play centre-half in place of Sunderland's Ray Daniel who, in 1956, was fined and suspended for one season by the Football Association for accepting under-the-counter money from his club.

The Czechs arrived in the Welsh capital three days before the game. Apart from asking the Welsh FA for 10 footballs for their training session the men from behind the Iron Curtain also requested a coach trip to the seaside, 300 postcards and stamps and information on how to buy English cigarettes.

Few were forecasting a Welsh victory. Not only were Wales below full strength but the Czechs, with players like left-back and captain Ladislav Novák, left-half Josef Masopust and centre-forward Vlastimil Bubnik, the latter also a world-famous ice hockey player, were seen as a genuine force in world football. The visitors also impressed their hosts with their pre-match preparations. In training they looked graceful and, typical for an East European side, highly efficient. After the players had finished their warm-up sessions the Czech trainer even tested the temperature of the bath water before the players jumped in.

"Czechoslovakia had taken over from Hungary as the best team in Europe," says Terry Medwin, Wales's outside-right that May evening. "They were very skillful. They didn't hit balls long. They were very patient and they were also a big side. They weren't a fast passing side, they preferred to keep possession."

A crowd of 50,000 packed into Ninian Park to see the first World Cup qualifying match. They did not leave disappointed. In a thrilling 90 minutes Vernon struck the only goal of the game after 73 minutes to put Wales in the Group Four driving seat.

"The Czechs played terrifically well at Cardiff but we just pipped them," recalls John Charles who played in defence alongside his younger brother Mel. Murphy, in fact, had no hesitation in using the new Juventus signing as a defender because he believed Charles was the best centre-half in the world and marvelled at the way he could head a ball 40 yards clear. "I didn't mind playing at the back. I played wherever they wanted me," adds Charles. "I was just pleased to play."

Wales, the underdogs despite the home advantage, dominated the first half-an-hour with Cliff Jones giving the Czech full-back, Jan Hertl, an uncomfortable time although debutant Webster was struggling to get the better of his marker, Jiri Cadek. With 20 minutes gone John Charles, being watched from the stand by his 'minder' and Juventus scout Gigi Peronace, saw a shot graze Bretislav Dolejsi's post. After that the Czechs began to settle down and test Jack Kelsey. At the start of the second-half they nearly took the lead but Jaroslav Borovicka, their inside-left, headed over the bar from just six yards.

"I consider that match as the best I ever played for Wales," says Jones. "Hertl was just the sort of full-back I liked playing against. He was strong and a good footballer, but he did not have a turn of speed so a push and sprint was usually enough to beat him." The winning goal came with 17 minutes remaining and somewhat against the run of play. Medwin nodded down Derek Tapscott's cross and there was Vernon, who at the time was doing his national service with the Royal Welch Fusiliers in Wrexham, to smack the ball past Dolejsi.

In the last 10 minutes the Czechs searched frantically for the equaliser but Kelsey made a string of stunning saves. "The Czechs were easily the cleverest side in the group but we soon discovered the Czech's skill with the ball was not matched by their shooting power. They weaved patterns and then ran slap into our steel-like defence," recalls Jones.

So Wales, despite all the pessimism beforehand, drew first blood in Group Four, but a demanding week now followed for Murphy's team – a week behind the Iron Curtain. Their next qualifier was against the East Germans, in Leipzig, on May 19. Then, seven days later, they would meet the Czechs once more, in Prague. For Wales, it was make-or-break time. If they could return home with three points then qualification would be virtually assured. However, on this trip to Eastern Europe the Welsh FA displayed its inexperience and naivety. Incredibly, just 12 players flew to Leipzig compared to 10 selectors. It would have been 11 but Milwyn Jenkins, a solicitor and the Welsh FA's chairman, was unable to travel due to High Court commitments. Murphy's dozen were Jack Kelsey, Mel Hopkins, Dai Thomas, Trevor Edwards, Mel Charles, Bill Harris, Dave Bowen, Reg Davies, Terry Medwin, Derek Tapscott, Roy Vernon and Cliff Jones. Among the 12 players one of them, Derek Tapscott, was nursing an ankle injury. John Charles, touring Holland with Leeds, was expected to boost the squad to 13, but he would arrive in Leipzig just two days before the match, via Amsterdam and Frankfurt. It was an unbelievable scenario. As the party left their training base in Weybridge, Surrey, for London Airport to catch the flight to Berlin, the non-playing staff, which included the selectors, Murphy (the manager), Jack Jones (the trainer) and Bill Hughes (the team doctor), outnumbered the playing staff 13–12. Wales would pay dearly for such short-sightedness.

"There were more selectors than players," remembers John Charles. "It was crazy. You've got to put the players first but with Wales it was the selectors first and the players second. One time we were playing abroad and there was one seat short on the plane. In the end it was one of the players who had to stay behind, not one of the selectors."

The Welsh party landed in Berlin and then made the four-hour trip to Leipzig, the second largest city in East Germany, by coach, passing through the Brandenburg Gate and Checkpoint Charlie which divided the capitalist West Berlin from the communist East. The selectors, however, did not travel with the players but were chauffeur-driven in Zis cars, the Zis being the Soviet answer to a limousine.

The squad stayed in the old-fashioned Astoria Hotel, right in the heart of Leipzig city centre. Again, the selectors had shown their inexperience. With little privacy – the players were pestered for tickets and autographs – and lots of noise, the Astoria was hardly the ideal base to focus on a crunch World Cup qualifier. "It wasn't a very good hotel," says Hopkins. "A bar of chocolate in the hotel room was considered a luxury. I would have classed it as two star, although for them it was probably five star." The hotel management handed their Welsh guests coupons which had to be presented in the dining-room to order food. The deprivation and fear prevalent in

East Germany left a deep impression on Hopkins. "People wouldn't talk to you out there. I noticed the East Germans had false teeth made of steel. There were special police everywhere, wandering around in suits. If you were taking photos they wanted to know what you were taking photos of."

Hopkins was not the only Welsh player rattled by what he saw in 1950s East Germany. "By looking around you wouldn't have known the war had ended," says Medwin. "Everything was so poorly done – the roads, the houses. I remember thinking how lucky I was living in Britain."

The venue for this Group Four match was the Zentralstadion, the country's showpiece stadium. It was East Germany's first ever competitive match and, coupled with the fact that the world's most expensive player, John Charles, would be on show, interest in the game was phenomenal – 110,000 tickets were sold although the organisers could have sold five times that amount.

This time Wales, thanks to their 1–0 win over Czechoslovakia 19 days earlier, were the favourites. East Germany's most respected football journalists, Willi Meisl and Erich Chemnitz, forecasted a Welsh win, so too did East Germany's manager Janos Gyarmati. Gyarmati, a Hungarian, said, "We are amateurs playing against professionals. I saw Wales beat the Czechs at Cardiff. I think Wales will finish top of the three countries and will proceed to the finals in Sweden." Gyarmati, a wily fox of a manager, may have been trying to install over-confidence in the Welsh camp since East Germany's recent record was good. In fact, they were unbeaten in two years.

Murphy made several changes to the side that beat the Czechs at Ninian Park. The team to face East Germany was: Kelsey (Arsenal), Edwards (Charlton), Hopkins (Tottenham), Harris (Middlesbrough), John Charles (Juventus), Bowen (Arsenal), Medwin (Tottenham), Tapscott (Arsenal), Mel Charles (Swansea Town), Vernon (Blackburn), Jones (Swansea Town). The big change was at centre-forward where Mel Charles replaced the ineffective Webster. Edwards had replaced Stitfall at right-back and Harris slotted in at right-half, the position vacated by Mel Charles.

"I was superstitious. I always ran out onto the field last," says Mel Charles. "For this game I came out of the changing room last and someone gave me a bunch of flowers. They were supposed to give them to John because he was the captain, but obviously they had just missed him or they mistook me for him. When the anthems were being played there I was holding these flowers not knowing what they were for. I turned to Dave Bowen and said, 'Dave, what do I do with them?' He said, 'I don't know. Just throw them into the crowd'.

That's what I did, I ran off the pitch and threw them at the crowd. Then John started playing hell with me. He was effing and blinding. Apparently the captains had to exchange the flowers before the kick-off and they had spent five minutes looking for the bunch I'd thrown away. But at least I won us a bit more support!"

Wales immediately seized control of the game and John Charles, with his very first touch, drew 110,000 gasps. From inside his penalty area Charles leapt and headed the ball clear. It went as far as the centre-circle. After just six minutes his brother, Mel, opened the scoring. The first Welsh victory on foreign soil was on the cards. Once again Medwin had a hand in the goal. He whipped in a cross, Tapscott miskicked but Charles was on hand to scramble the ball home. A wall of silence greeted the goal. The East German crowd was stunned. There were no Welsh supporters inside the vast Zentralstadion – 100 Royal Welch Fusiliers, based in West Berlin, tried to attend this World Cup qualifier but the Soviet authorities refused to issue them with visas.

Wales's domination lasted only another nine minutes. Then, Murphy's side went to pieces. At right-back Edwards was having a nightmare against the German outside-left, Gunther Wirth, who was considered one of the best left-wingers in Europe, while Bowen and Tapscott did not appear one hundred per cent fit. Midway through the first-half the East Germans cancelled out Charles's early goal. Lothar Meyer, the German right-winger, beat Hopkins and, with the Welsh defence standing still, Wirth fired home the equaliser. The Zentralstadion erupted.

The second-half started 10 minutes later because the half-time break lasted 25 minutes. The Russian referee, Nikolai Latychev, explained the delay after the match. "The stadium is so big it takes five minutes to walk to the dressing room and five minutes to walk back to the arena." Despite the extended break Wales were just as lethargic as they were in the first 45 minutes. On the hour the inevitable happened. Willi Troger, the one-handed centre-forward, put the Germans 2–1 ahead. Troger, it was later said, lost his right hand in an industrial accident. Even with this disadvantage the 29–year-old still gave John Charles a torrid time in defence. "I remember feeling sorry for him and maybe I shouldn't have done," recalls Charles. "When I saw him I thought, 'Bloody hell! He's only got one arm. I don't want to hurt him'. But he was able to look after himself. I wasn't able to shoulder-barge him though! Seriously, he had a very good game. He was very quick." In the last 15 minutes, in a desperate attempt to snatch an equaliser, Murphy moved Charles to centre-forward but even Big John made no difference. The match ended 2–1 and Wales's qualification hopes had suffered a severe setback.

"We were OK until half-time but we didn't play well in the second-half. " admits Medwin. "We tried to get a point but we were losing possession easily and we were sluggish while the Germans raised their game in the second-half. It was probably because we had just finished a long season back home, but there were no excuses really. Jimmy was a bit uptight after this match."

The East German Press, which had sung Wales's praises before the 90 minutes, were disappointed with their Group Four rivals. The *Sportecho Berlin* newspaper afterwards said, "We were delighted to win but how Wales shocked us by their poor form. They appeared to be without fight."

Murphy and his players returned to the Astoria to lick their wounds. In four days time they would fly to Prague to prepare for what had become a decisive qualifier against the Czechs. It was a match Wales had to win if they were to have any chance of reaching the 1958 World Cup. The flight from East Berlin to Czechoslovakia, in a 48–seater Dakota plane, was a memorable one. "I put my seat-belt on and it came off at the side," recalls Hopkins. "I was very apprehensive about the journey. I remember the landing as well. We landed on a dirt-track! When the plane landed I looked out of the window and all this mud flew onto the glass. It was as if we landed in a field."

Wales would now pay for flying over such a thin squad. After the East Germany match the players had dropped like ninepins, Bowen with a back strain, Tapscott, who had spent the last minutes of the game limping badly, with a bad ankle while Reg Davies, the frail inside-right, was bedridden with a sore throat.

For the selectors 13 had indeed proved an unlucky number. The number of fit players was now 10 – not enough to make a football team. The red-faced officials now had to contact replacements in Britain and then fly them to Prague. The first target was Sunderland centre-half Ray Daniel but the selectors, anxious to cover-up their ineptitude, refused to inform the travelling Press corps of his sudden inclusion.

The Press, however, did find out about Daniel, and the Welsh FA's secretive behaviour generated tension between the selectors and the reporters. "They didn't tell us and they nearly made us look foolish," recalls Jim Hill, the Cardiff-born sports writer who covered Wales's Iron Curtain trip for the *Daily Express*. "It caused a lot of bad feeling and after that we decided to hammer the selectors in our reports. We found out about Daniel because our newsdesks back

home had heard stories coming from Sunderland that Daniel was flying to Czechoslovakia. Herbert Powell (secretary of the Welsh FA)
had no relationship at all with the Press. If you asked him a question
he would just say 'You know you shouldn't ask me questions like
that'. That was the way Powell treated the Press."

Daniel's call-up was a surprise since he had not played football for
an entire season. The FA had banned Daniel from playing the
1956/57 season after he was found to be one of the Sunderland players who had accepted illegal payments from the North East club. The
ban, though, was lifted on May 17 – nine days before the Czech
game.

Daniel arrived in Prague with a brand new pair of football boots.
As Tapscott explains, this was not a good thing. "The boots in those
days were thick and heavy-leathered with hard toes and knock-in
studs. It would take you about 12 months to break them in. They
were very, very uncomfortable. We would put them in soapy water to
soften them up and then stuff them with brown paper so they would
fill out." Daniel's broken-in boots were kept in the boot room at
Roker Park, Sunderland's ground. When the SOS from Prague
came, Daniel was hundreds of miles away, on holiday in his native
Swansea. He telegraphed Sunderland and asked them to send his
boots to London where he could pick them up before catching the
plane. Sunderland sent him boots, but they turned out to be new
ones.

"Imagine my thoughts. I was out of training, my country needed
me and I was having to play in a pair of boots that needed weeks of
breaking in," recalled Daniel afterwards. "I arrived in Prague feeling
rather depressed. I tried the boots on in training and they hurt. I
borrowed some from John Charles, but they were not my size so I
persevered with the new ones."

Within days of joining his team-mates at the Hotel Paris the centre-
half was in considerable discomfort. After a training session, his first
for seven months, Daniel was so stiff he needed a brine bath. The
boots, not surprisingly, were also troubling him. After two days of
wearing them he had a huge corn on one of his feet. The corn was cut
off and a swab was needed to stop the heavy flow of blood. An Olympic legend came to Daniel's aid. Emil Zátopek, who won three gold
medals in the 1952 Olympic Games in Helsinki – in the 5,000 metres,
10,000 metres and the marathon – was also staying in the Hotel Paris
and had befriended the Welsh squad. He fashioned special pads to go
inside Daniel's boots to try and make them more comfortable.

Three days after Daniel's arrival the selectors sent another SOS,
this time for Swansea Town's young centre-forward Des Palmer.

Tapscott's ankle had not improved so a replacement was needed at inside-right. The replacement was Palmer who had never before played for Wales. Palmer recalls the moment he discovered he was on his way to the Czech capital. "I was living in Swansea. It was the end of the season and I stopped off at my local newsagent. The shopkeeper told me 'You've been selected!' and that's how I found out. Joe Sykes (the Swansea trainer) brought my boots to my house and gave me all the details. I put some things in a case and got the train to London from where I flew to Plague. I was met at the airport by Jimmy Murphy and Jack Jones. But when the team flew back home I had to come back separately because I wasn't part of the original booking. I came back with the golfer Dai Rees which was nice."

Palmer landed in Prague the day before the match. Looking back," he says, "the whole thing was dreadfully arranged." Jim Hill adds, "It was a farce. To take so many officials and then have to send for players was farcical." The Press would blame the selectors for the heavy defeat at the hands of the rampant Czechs.

Murphy made, or rather was forced to make, several changes to the side that faced East Germany. Mel Charles dropped back to right-half, his favourite position at club level, and brother John was named as centre-forward, Murphy finally realising Wales needed the Gentle Giant in attack far more than in defence. Bill Harris replaced Bowen at left-half and Swansea Town's Dai Thomas replaced Edwards at right-back. Daniel, plagued by blistered feet despite Zátopek's efforts, was picked at centre-half and Palmer at inside-right. The team that faced Czechoslovakia was: Kelsey (Arsenal), Thomas (Swansea Town), Hopkins (Tottenham), Mel Charles (Swansea Town), Daniel (Sunderland), Harris (Middlesbrough), Medwin (Tottenham), Palmer (Swansea Town), John Charles (Juventus), Vernon (Blackburn), Jones (Swansea Town).

Amazingly, the Czech Press were pessimistic about their nation's chances. Perhaps paying too much respect to the result at Ninian Park earlier that month, they predicted another Welsh victory. They were made to look foolish. Wales, inside the Stadion Juliska, the home of Dukla Prague, produced a display even more dire than the one against East Germany. The rout started after 21 minutes when poor Daniel scored a spectacular own goal. Kasimir Gajdos, the right-winger who ran Hopkins ragged, crossed and Daniel, who otherwise had a fine match, headed the ball past Kelsey. While the jubilant Czech players celebrated Daniel buried his head in his hands. Tadeas Kraus, the outside-left, added a splendid second to kill off the lacklustre visitors. The match finished 2–0 but, as Mervyn Thomas wrote in the *South Wales Echo*, it could so easily have been 6–0.

This second successive defeat meant Wales had little chance of qualifying for Sweden. The only hope was that East Germany and Czechoslovakia, who would now play their two games, beat each other and then for Wales to score an avalanche of goals against the Germans in Cardiff in September. But with the Czechs in such scintillating form the chances of an upset were remote, to say the least.

Just three of Murphy's players could walk off the Juliska field with any credit that day – Kelsey, Harris and Daniel. The latter had played through the pain barrier to keep the brilliant Czechs at bay. As Tapscott recalls, "Ray was in agony playing with those new boots, especially when you remember that in those days the ball was much heavier than it is today. In the last 10–15 minutes he took off his boots and just played in his socks. That's how much pain he was in." Palmer, the other SOS player, had a poor match and was always second-best to Masopust. "Ray and Des were not really fit," says Tapscott. "The season was over, they hadn't played for a fortnight and in Ray's case, much longer. They had about a day's training before the game and they couldn't do too much in case they pulled any muscles."

Murphy's team had been well and truly outclassed as the Czechs avenged their May Day defeat in the Welsh capital. "They were an excellent side, one of the top four in Europe," says Hopkins. "They pushed the ball around lovely and it was a hard game for us. They were the better side."

There was an air of anti-climax for Wales's final qualifier against the East Germans on September 25. As expected, the Czechs won both their matches against their communist neighbours, 3–1 in Prague and 4–1 in Leipzig, and so booked their place in Sweden as European Group Four champions. The Wales-East Germany fixture was now only a battle for second-place.

The Welsh team read: Vearncombe (Cardiff City), Thomas (Swansea Town), Hopkins (Tottenham), Harris (Middlesbrough) Mel Charles (Swansea Town), Bowen (Arsenal), Len Allchurch (Swansea Town), Davies (Newcastle) Palmer (Swansea Town), Vernon (Blackburn), Jones (Swansea Town). Graham Vearncombe replaced Kelsey who was ruled out with a knee injury. In attack Palmer, deputising for John Charles, won his second cap. Charles, now the star at Juventus, relied on the goodwill of his new employers when it came to playing for his country. On this occasion, a meaningless affair, the Italians refused to risk their expensive import.

Charles, though, was hardly missed as Palmer bagged a hat-trick in a 4–1 victory. His first came after 36 minutes, then two more followed in seven minutes. From Cliff Jones's cross East German goalkeeper Gunther Busch punched into his own net before Palmer notched his second of the night. In the second-half the Germans pulled one back when Mel Charles, emulating Daniel, put through his own net but it was Palmer who had the final say in Wales's biggest win since March 1952 when Northern Ireland lost 3–0 in Swansea. "Everything went right for me against the Germans," recalls Palmer. "I felt I could have had a couple more that night. I was really flying."

When, at 7.15pm, English referee Reg Leafe blew the final whistle, the players applauded the Ninian Park crowd and then trudged off the pitch. They were convinced their World Cup ambitions had ended for at least another four years. So too were the Welsh supporters. They did not know it then but two months later this apparently meaningless win would have huge significance.

On November 25, 1957, FIFA held an emergency meeting in Zürich. The Asia-Africa section was in disarray because the Arab teams refused to play Israel. The origins of Arab-Israeli hostility date back to 1947 when, after the United Nations partitioned Palestine into an Arab state and a Jewish state, the first Arab-Israeli war broke out. The battles stopped in 1949, but in 1956 a second Arab-Israel war started over border conflicts, most notably the Egyptian-controlled Gaza Strip. Although the war lasted only months and Israeli forces withdrew from the Gaza Strip in March 1957, the ceasefire was an uneasy one.

To decide who played Israel for one of the 16 places in Sweden FIFA organised a draw involving most of the runners-up. Wales, enjoying an ill-deserved slice of luck bearing in mind their amateurish preparations for the Iron Curtain matches, were picked. After the low-key draw in Switzerland, Murphy said, "Wales has got a second chance of qualifying for the World Cup finals in Sweden and you can take it from me the lads are going to grasp the opportunity with both hands."

The play-off was a two-leg affair. The first leg would be played in Tel Aviv on January 15, 1958, and the second in Cardiff on February 5. "To tell you the truth we didn't even know Israel had a team," says Mel Charles. "The only Israel I ever read about was the one in the Bible."

Stuart Williams, the West Bromwich Albion defender who was not selected for the previous qualifying games but who played both games against Israel, recalls, "When we left Britain it was wet and freezing cold. We arrived in Israel wearing warm clothes and it was boiling hot when we landed in Tel Aviv. I think it was around 80 degrees." The extreme changes in climate affected Vearncombe, the reserve goalkeeper. During the team's first training session inside the half-built Ramat Gan Stadium, the venue for the match, he collapsed and had to be carried into the cool of the dressing room to recover. "We were doing some exercises and someone heard a body falling," says Williams. "We turned round and it was Graham." Alan Harrington, the Cardiff City full-back, also remembers the incident. "Jimmy had us running around the pitch and suddenly Graham keeled over. We carried him to the dressing room and after about 15 minutes he was all right. The doctor said it was the climate."

It was a strong Wales XI that faced the Israelis, whose average age was just 23. Juventus had agreed to release John Charles for both games and Ivor Allchurch, too, had returned to the fray after missing the previous six internationals through injury. The Ramat Gan Stadium, on the outskirts of Tel Aviv, did not impress the Welsh players. "The road leading to the stadium was basically a dirt-track," recalls Medwin. Mel Charles remembers visiting the ground before the match. "They were still building it at the time. I saw all these oxen pulling concrete blocks. We were told they had just put the turf down a week before the game. After 10 minutes of football it became like a bloody ploughed field! It was like a bomb site." And Williams adds, "The dressing rooms were non-existent. Before the game we changed at the hotel and after it we jumped straight onto the bus and had a shower back at our hotel."

The Israelis began work on the Ramat Gan Stadium in 1950 but it was still far from completion. There were mounds of grass behind each goal and only one side of the ground contained seating, the other side was more or less open. A deep moat surrounded the pitch and barbed wire was scattered all over the ground while the pitch was as bumpy as a cobbled street. Nevertheless, all 36,000 tickets had been snapped up by the Israeli public and because of the traffic congestion caused by the match the Welsh team arrived 15 minutes late.

Murphy named the following side to face Israel: Kelsey (Arsenal), Williams (West Brom), Hopkins (Tottenham), Harrington (Cardiff City), Mel Charles (Swansea Town), Bowen (Arsenal), Len Allchurch (Swansea Town), John Charles (Juventus), Medwin (Tottenham), Ivor Allchurch (Swansea Town), Cliff Jones (Swansea Town). Curiously, this Welsh side contained two sets of brothers, the Charleses and the Allchurches.

Wales took a huge leap towards Sweden by winning the away leg 2–0. The Israelis surprised the visitors with their tough tackling, but they had no answer to Ivor Allchurch who scored a peach of a goal from 25 yards shortly before half-time. Bowen scored the second after 68 minutes, another long-range effort from 20 yards which surprised Israel's acrobatic goalkeeper Yaacov Chodoroff.

As forecast, Wales had a comfortable ride against the Middle East amateurs. "They had some skillful players," says Williams, "but as an attacking force they were practically nil." Medwin recalls, "They were fit but they didn't have much ability." Hopkins agrees with Medwin. "Israel had one or two useful players but they were a very naive side. Football was not their sport. Their temperament was not good, they were very excitable, and tactically they were naive. They would follow the ball and get out of position. They didn't cover well, either."

When they returned home, each team member was presented with a box of oranges, a gift from the Cardiff Jewry. "I heard a knock on my door. When I opened it there was someone standing with a box full of these huge oranges," recalls Hopkins, who at the time lived in Palmer's Green, north London. "The box was quite big. It was two feet long and about two feet wide. The oranges stunk the house out for weeks."

The second-leg in Cardiff three weeks later was a mere formality. The Israeli squad arrived in Cardiff with a special supporter, the beautiful cabaret singer Aviva Revah. Her distracting presence annoyed Israel's head of selectors, Sam Socher, who demanded to know who had invited her on the trip. Tamfield's Diary, a gossip column in the *Daily Mail*, romantically linked Revah, who was married to a nose-flute player, to Wales captain Dave Bowen, who was married himself. It claimed Bowen had met her during a pre-match function in Tel Aviv, which he attended with Mel and John Charles, and that he had invited over for the second-leg. The allegations incensed Bowen. As journalist Jim Hill, who was a friend of Bowen, recalls, "Dave was a lovely guy and this was not the sort of thing he would do. He denied everything like hell. He was hopping mad over these rumours." It was later revealed that Chodoroff, Israel's star player despite being a goalkeeper, had lured Revah to Britain.

The Welsh team picked for the second-leg was: Kelsey (Arsenal), Williams (West Brom), Hopkins (Tottenham), Harrington (Cardiff City), Mel Charles (Swansea Town), Bowen (Arsenal), Medwin (Tottenham), Hewitt (Cardiff City), John Charles (Juventus), Ivor Allchurch (Swansea Town), Cliff Jones (Swansea Town). Hewitt, an inside-right and making his international debut, was the only change from the side that played in Tel Aviv.

Israel's already slim hopes were washed away with the heavy rain the night before the match. "The Israelis won't like this wet ground," Gigi Peronace, Charles's ubiquitous escort, told Kelsey in the dressing room.

It was Kelsey's opposite number, Chodoroff, who stole the show. Dressed in black the Israeli prevented his country losing by a cricket score, pulling off save after save as Wales piled on the pressure. Chodoroff, in fact, kept the scoreline at 0–0 until well into the second-half. Then, with just over 20 minutes left, the turning point came – the Israeli and John Charles collided while both jumping for a high ball. Chodoroff came off worse. Charles dusted himself down and jogged back upfield. As for Chodoroff, he suffered concussion, a broken nose and a sprained shoulder, but he had to carry on. With Chodoroff dazed Wales score twice, first a marvellous solo effort from Allchurch, who fired home almost from the by-line, and then Jones, who converted a Medwin pass following a wonderful defence-splitting ball from the impressive Hewitt. For Jones, the goal was timely. He was expected to leave Swansea for a Division One club, probably Tottenham where he would join fellow Welshmen Hopkins and Medwin. "The second meeting at Ninian Park," says Jones, "was called The Auction, because there were so many managers there watching me."

The second-leg ended 2–0 with Wales winning 4–0 on aggregate. After the final whistle Chodoroff was taken to nearby St David's Hospital for treatment. The clash with 14 stone Big John had clearly affected him since he thought Israel had lost 4–0 and not 2–0. He also spoke to the nurses in Hebrew, believing he was home in Israel. As for Murphy and the Welsh players, they celebrated until the early hours at a banquet at the Park Hotel. "We had a good session there," recalls Mel Charles. "But there was no champagne. The Welsh FA couldn't afford it! We had a pint of beer each instead."

Wales were off to the 1958 World Cup in Sweden. As representatives of Asia-Africa.

CHAPTER TWO

THE TEAM-TALK KING

FEBRUARY 6, 1958. It was the day after the Wales-Israel match. Jimmy Murphy had arrived in Manchester's London Road Station from Cardiff shortly before 4pm. Carrying a box of oranges, a present from the Israeli FA, he summoned a taxi to Old Trafford. There he was due to welcome Matt Busby, Manchester United's manager, and his players from their successful European Cup trip in Belgrade.

On arrival, Murphy climbed the stairs that led to his office – known affectionately by United staff as Murphy's Bar.

He was smiling broadly. After all, Wales were going to Sweden and Murphy's beloved United were on course for a remarkable treble – the League, the FA Cup and the European Cup.

Life could not be sweeter. He had his hand on the door handle when Alma George, Matt Busby's distraught secretary, told him the shattering news – "The plane has crashed at Munich!"

An hour earlier, in snowy Bavaria, Flight 609 – a twin-engine BEA Elizabethan airliner carrying the United party – skidded on the slush-covered runway and ploughed into a building at Munich Airport where it had refuelled en route from Belgrade. It crashed after its third attempt at take-off.

Murphy stepped into his office and cried for 20 minutes. For the next 12 hours he sat at his desk making desperate telephone calls, trying to find out what happened, who was injured, who had survived, who was dead. That glorious afternoon at Ninian Park was no longer important. It was as if the Israel match had never even happened.

As the night wore on, the news Murphy dreaded started to filter through. Seven of the Busby Babes were dead – Roger Byrne, Eddie Colman, Tommy Taylor, Geoff Bent, Mark Jones, Bill Whelan, David Pegg. There were 10 survivors from the United party but two of them, the brilliant Duncan Edwards and Matt Busby were fighting for their lives. Edwards would need a kidney machine, Busby was in an oxygen tent.

Busby, a friend of Murphy's since their playing days two decades earlier, would eventually pull through but a fortnight later 21-year-old Edwards died from his injuries.

What should have been a night of joy and celebration following the Welsh win in Cardiff had turned into the worst possible nightmare. The Manchester United team Murphy and Busby had spent 13 years carefully building had been wiped out in the ice and cold of southern Germany.

Murphy took on the harrowing task of notifying the players' families of their loss. He did not reach his home in Whalley Range until 4am. As soon as he arrived he poured himself a drink, not the expected champagne to toast Wales's qualification for the 1958 World Cup, but an entire bottle of Scotch to mourn the death of his team. As Busby's assistant, Murphy had nurtured and groomed them. They were his boys.

"It must have been devastating for Jimmy," says Terry Medwin. "One of his jobs at United was to go and meet the parents and kids, and he had helped bring those players through."

Later that morning, after a sleepless night, Murphy was flying to Munich to see the survivors. During the grim journey he reflected on how his life had almost certainly been saved by that FIFA draw in Zürich three months earlier. Fate had decided that his close friend Bert Whalley, one of United's scouts and coaches, should replace him on that doomed European Cup trip.

Whalley, who sat next to Busby, was one of the 23 people – including club officials and journalists – who died in the tragedy. Had Wales not been chosen to face the Israelis, had one of the other six nations been pulled out of the Jules Rimet Trophy, then Murphy would have been on that Elizabethan airliner instead. And Murphy, as assistant manager, would have sat next to Busby.

After three distressing days touring the wards of the Rechts der Isar Hospital in Munich, he returned to Manchester. Nine players had survived. Until Busby had fully recovered, the Welshman was put in charge at Old Trafford and he had the unenviable task of rebuilding a devastated side.

Since the crash four days earlier he had kept a brave face in an attempt to maintain morale at Old Trafford, especially among the two players who had escaped unscathed from the horrific crash, goalkeeper Harry Gregg and defender Bill Foulkes.

Murphy was a master at hiding his feelings, a legacy of growing up in the hardship of the Rhondda Valley during the Twenties. However, the day he received a list of United's remaining professional players, Murphy broke down. "They're just kids," he murmured.

"There's nothing left." There and then the full extent of the tragedy hit him and he collapsed in tears. Of the Munich survivors only Gregg, Foulkes, Bobby Charlton and Welsh teenager Ken Morgans, would play that season.

Murphy, however, did a remarkable job as acting manager. Nobody would have been surprised to see United capitulate after losing so many first-team players in one swoop, but Murphy gradually pieced together the jigsaw. Welsh international Colin Webster, one of the reserves who became a United regular after the Munich disaster, watched in amazement as Murphy inspired the players to reach the FA Cup final three months later.

"Murphy was a workaholic," recalls Webster. "He never seemed to get tired. After the crash at Munich we never saw him go to bed, he was always at the ground. Whenever I was there he was there. He never showed his feelings. To be honest, I think he was too busy to show any feelings. He was always on the go."

Soon after taking Busby's chair, Murphy made two inspirational signings – Ernie Taylor, an inside-forward, from Blackpool, and Stan Crowther, a hard-tackling wing-half, from Aston Villa.

Murphy remembered Taylor's remarkable performance for Blackpool in the 1953 FA Cup final, known as 'the Matthews Final'. But, in Murphy's view, the real hero of Blackpool's triumph that day was not Stanley Matthews but midfield general Taylor.

Crowther's signing showed Murphy's persistence. For days he had tried to coax Crowther to Manchester but the Villa star was reluctant to move. In the end, Crowther put pen to paper, just hours before making his United debut in the FA Cup fifth-round tie against Sheffield Wednesday.

Murphy also tried to sign Hungarian legend Ferenc Puskas from Real Madrid, but there was an obstacle. Puskas was earning £800 a-week at Real whereas the maximum weekly wage in English football was £17 a-week. "You know the real reason Puskas didn't join United?" teases Webster. "Because Murph said he was only one-footed!"

For the rest of the season Murphy took the team to Blackpool for training. "After Munich he managed to keep everyone's mind on the football. Murphy made sure we were hardly ever at Old Trafford because there were too many distractions," adds Webster. "Outside Manchester we all felt normal, but when we were in the city we were reminded of what had happened because people kept coming up to us and talking about it."

What Webster admired most about Murphy, though, was the way he could motivate his players. "He would foam at the mouth and curse the opposition. He would shout, 'You can beat this lot of crap!' By the end of his talk you wanted to run through a brick wall for him."

During training, too, Murphy was a force to be reckoned with.

"He would play in a practice match and he'd kick you, no problem," remembers Webster. "He'd go over the top as well, onto your shin or knee. If you tried to get him back he'd say, 'Don't, I'm an old man. Save it for Saturday.' He used to take us to play golf quite a lot. If we didn't play he'd still make us walk round the course.

"If he didn't like you that was that, end of story. I remember once when the commentator, David Coleman (sports presenter for the BBC), came into the United dressing room. I think it was at Aston Villa's ground. Murphy grabbed him by the arse and collar and threw him out into the corridor. That was Murphy to a tee. He might change his mind about someone but it would take an awful lot."

Murphy had arrived at Old Trafford in 1946, after he had survived fighting the Germans in North Africa. Busby, on military duty himself, had been impressed by Murphy's rousing team talk to a bunch of soldiers at a sports centre in the southern Italian port of Bari. He invited him to become his deputy at United.

"If you fancy a job when you are demobbed, Jimmy, come and look me up at Old Trafford," said the Scot. When he returned home Murphy did just that.

Busby had remembered Murphy's never-say-die approach when they were both footballers during the Thirties, Busby with United, Murphy with West Bromwich Albion.

Everyone at Old Trafford knew the story of Murphy in the 1935 FA Cup Final. West Brom were losing 4–1 to Sheffield Wednesday. In the dying minutes the Midlanders pulled a goal back but at 4–2 it was all over. Murphy, however, ran into the net, picked up the ball, ran back to the centre-spot and slammed the ball down. The stocky Welshman had not given up.

A wonderful motivator and hard taskmaster, Murphy's greatest gift was to make the most from limited resources. Wales could boast very few world-class players but Murphy did have three or four. They were goalkeeper Jack Kelsey, winger Cliff Jones and two forwards, Ivor Allchurch and John Charles. Murphy built the Welsh team around them.

He did the same while he was acting manager of United. The new-look Red Devils, a mixture of reserves playing out of position and hurried new signings, fitted around the talented trio who had survived the crash, Gregg, Foulkes and Charlton.

United's league challenge faded and they were knocked out of the European Cup by Milan. Nevertheless, Murphy pulled off the feat of the season by leading his team of misfits all the way to the FA Cup final where they faced a Bolton Wanderers side spearheaded by the great Nat Lofthouse. There was no fairy-tale ending. United went down 2–0, both goals scored by Lofthouse.

"What he achieved in those months after Munich was fantastic," says Webster. "I don't think Busby could have done it. I don't think there were many people who could have done it. But then again, Murphy was a one-off."

What effect the Munich air disaster had on Murphy's duties as Wales manager remains debatable. Murphy was, post-Munich, spending up to 18 hours a day at Old Trafford. Whalley had died in the crash, so too did Tom Curry, the team trainer, and Walter Crickmer, the club secretary while Busby was recovering in Germany. Murphy was, in effect, doing the job of four men. He was running the biggest club in England almost single-handed.

Nor did he sleep at night. Murphy admitted that as soon as his head hit his pillow he could only think about the players who had died in the crash. As a result he was not as well-prepared for the World Cup as he could have been.

The get-together in London just days before the flight to Sweden in June was the first time Murphy had spent any quality time with the Welsh players since the Israel match at Cardiff in the first week of February.

Murphy had thrown himself body and soul into dealing with the problems at United. There had been no time to watch any of Wales's first-round opponents, Hungary, Mexico and Sweden, nor any of the likely teams Wales would face in the quarter-finals – if, by some chance, they did reach that stage.

"Not knowing anything about the other countries," admits Cliff Jones, "did not exactly fill us with confidence but it wasn't Jimmy's fault."

James Patrick Murphy was born in Pentre in the Rhondda Valley. His mother, from Pembrokeshire, had high hopes her son would become a schoolteacher. His Irish father, a pit repairer in a nearby colliery, was certain he would join his five brothers working down a mine. But Murphy fell in love with football and on the concrete playground of Pentre School he would play football with a screwed-up newspaper. His ambition was to play for Cardiff City.

In 1924, Murphy starred for Wales Schoolboys against England in the pouring rain at Ninian Park. Wales won 2–1 and after that the teenager waited for the call to join City. It never came.

Instead a call came from West Bromwich Albion who had heard good things about Murphy following his second schoolboys international against Scotland at Hampden Park. Soon Murphy was on his way to the West Midlands.

During the Thirties, Murphy, who had been converted to wing-half from inside-forward, emerged as one of Wales's finest players. The Welsh selectors, who had to find a replacement for Cardiff City's retiring Fred Keenor, decided to take a look at Murphy in a league match between Albion and Aston Villa in 1933.

Murphy, who had got wind he was being watched, had to mark Billy Walker, one of the best inside-forwards in the game. Walker often made fools of defenders but on this day he got no change from Murphy who reduced Walker to a demoralised heap and helped inspire Albion to a 3–1 win. Murphy was in the Welsh team to face Northern Ireland at Wrexham.

It was the start of a glittering international career. During his six years as a Wales player Murphy, part of the formidable back line which included Tommy Griffiths, of Wrexham, and Dai Richards, of Wolves, won the Home Championship on three occasions including the Triple Crown in 1933/34 when Wales beat England, Scotland and Northern Ireland. It was Welsh football's golden era.

So in 1957, when the Welsh selectors were looking for the right man to lead Wales in the forthcoming World Cup qualifying campaign, it was natural Murphy's name should be mentioned. He had been one of his country's finest pre-war players and, for 11 years, he had been assistant manager at Manchester United. He had helped Busby win two League championships and an FA Cup.

Murphy was also being highly praised for developing the talents of United young players, the Busby Babes, not least Duncan Edwards, who, at 17 years and eight months, had become the youngest player ever to wear the English shirt.

"If Murphy hadn't been at Old Trafford, the Busby Babes would never have existed," claims Webster. "Murphy brought them in, at least 80 per cent of them. He camped outside Duncan Edwards's home and slipped his dad the odd bottle of whisky so he would join United."

To sign Tommy Taylor he brought with him, to the astonishment of Cardiff City manager Cyril Spiers who was also trying to buy Taylor, a Catholic priest. This, Murphy believed, would show Taylor's parents that Manchester United was a responsible club. It worked. Taylor chose United. Eddie Colman, David Pegg, Mark Jones – they, too, were all Murphy's boys.

"They used to say the families would make their boys sign for

Murphy so they could get rid of him!" says Webster. "At United, Busby was the figurehead, the diplomat. Murph was the dog who chased everything. He was the man the players saw before Busby. If you had a problem you'd see Murph first. A couple of times I was furious with Busby and demanded to see him. Then Murph would talk to me. 'Do you want a beer?' he'd say. Before I knew it, I was leaving his office and I'd forgotten what I wanted to see Busby about. That's the effect Murphy had on us."

Murphy was announced as Wales's first ever permanent manager in March 1957, just two months before the crucial World Cup qualifier against Czechoslovakia in Cardiff. He had managed Wales on a match-for-match basis against Scotland, a 2–2 draw in Cardiff, and England, a 3–1 defeat at Wembley. Even though Wales failed to win either match, the selectors were impressed with his work. He replaced Walley Barnes who had now joined the BBC as a commentator.

Murphy, a patriot, jumped at the chance to manage his country although few envied him his new role. He inherited a team on its last legs, a team which now expected defeat. Since 1952, when Wales shared the Home Championship with England, the men in red had played 22 matches. They won three, drew four and lost no less than 15.

Murphy was under no illusions. A mountain had to be climbed if Wales were to reach Sweden. He wasted no time in reshaping the team.

The great full-back Alf Sherwood was past his prime while Ron Burgess and Roy Paul, two wonderful wing-backs, had also finished at international level. Burgess had been appointed manager of Swansea Town, Paul had left Manchester City to join Worcester City in the Southern League. To make matters worse, Murphy was forced to exclude centre-forward Trevor Ford who was shunned by the football establishment for writing a controversial autobiography.

Murphy looked to the emerging players to take Wales to the World Cup, men like Cliff Jones, the two Mels – Charles and Hopkins – Ivor Allchurch, Jack Kelsey and Terry Medwin.

"He changed the whole set-up," says Webster. "In the past, the selectors would decide everything, who played and where. But when Murphy took over he told them, 'I pick the team!'"

During meetings with the selectors at the FAW's headquarters in Wrexham, what Murphy said usually went. If he wanted a new player in the team, or if he thought a player should change positions, the selectors granted his wish.

But even the no-nonsense hard-man from the South Wales

Valleys occasionally lost out to the high-preaching selectors. Ford, for instance, remained in exile even though Murphy rated him one of the best forwards in the game. He reckoned the Welsh attack of Allchurch, Ford and John Charles was the best he had ever seen, but on some matters the selectors just would not budge. The issue of Ford was one of them.

The Welsh players soon took to the man from Old Trafford. Murphy, who enjoyed the odd glass of whisky and cigarette, was a fast talker with boundless energy and bagfuls of charm. He went down a treat with a squad low on morale and self-belief.

"He wasn't one for tactics. He was a great motivator. He would give these amazing team-talks before a game," recalls Mel Charles. The team-talk he remembers best took place before the World Cup qualifying match against East Germany at Cardiff. "Look lads!" shouted Murphy, pointing vaguely in the direction of the East German dressing room, "This lot bombed your mothers and fathers!" It was not subtle, it was not sporting, but it worked. Wales won 4–1.

"Jimmy gave it to you straight and the players liked him for that. He never went on about tactics and he never worried about the other team," adds Charles. "When I joined Arsenal, Ron Greenwood was there as a coach and he was a great one for talking tactics, but players would fall asleep listening to him. He would go on about "marking space" and "blind side runs" but with Jimmy there was none of that fancy stuff. He let us play our own game. All he wanted us to do was to clear our penalty area and be direct going forward."

No player benefitted from the Murphy regime more than Mel Charles. Under Barnes, the Swansea Town player had been moved around like a chess piece, from right-half to centre-half, from left-half to centre-forward to inside-forward. But under Murphy, he established himself as an accomplished centre-half. "Pelé picked me as the best centre-half in the World Cup," says Charles, proudly.

By his own admission Murphy was no theorist. "I don't believe in blackboards and I don't believe in FA handbooks," he once said. "I'm a practical man through and through." His methods were based on discipline, hard work and good man-management.

"He was good at team meetings but he'd also have a quiet word with certain players if they needed geeing up," recalls Terry Medwin. "He wasn't one for having a go at one player in front of everyone else. If he was angry about something he would have a go at every-one, but the players who weren't doing what Jimmy wanted knew who they were.

"He was hard when he had to be but he could also be very soft. As

long as you gave your best on the pitch he didn't mind about anything else. I remember six-a-sides with Jimmy. We'd finish playing
only when he had scored the winning goal! He was a very competitive
bloke. Players often respect coaches without enjoying their company, but everyone was always pleased to be with Jimmy because he
was such a pleasant man."

Wales became a force again under Murphy. Even though they lost
in Czechoslovakia and East Germany, both sides – and they were impressive sides – were well beaten in Cardiff. Although things were far
from perfect, Wales, thanks to some tips borrowed from Old
Trafford, were on the mend.

"We all thought the world of Jimmy Murphy," says Stuart
Williams. "He was very approachable, he was very passionate and he
would transfer that passion to us. He would spit fire and sawdust
during his team-talks. He would run down the opposition and, using
a fair share of bad language, he would say we were good players in
our own right. Jimmy wasn't, how could you say, a quietly spoken
bloke."

To halt the slide, the first thing Murphy did was to build a solid
and settled defence. He was a great admirer of Herbert Chapman, the
hugely successful Arsenal manager of the Thirties, whose motto was,
'If our opponents don't score, they can't beat us.'

Kelsey was an automatic choice in goal. In front of him, Murphy
plumped for Mel Charles at centre-half, Williams at right-back, Mel
Hopkins at left-back, Dave Bowen, who he would make captain, at
left-half, and Derrick Sullivan at right-half.

In Sweden, the Welsh rearguard was one of the best in the tournament, conceding only four goals in five games. Only winners Brazil
would boast a better defensive record although Murphy was to go as
far as saying the Welsh defence was *the* best defence of the 1958
World Cup.

But the headache was who would score the goals. The answer, as
far as Murphy was concerned, John Charles. Since he made his international debut in 1950, Charles had played more games at centre-
half than he did at centre-forward. Yet this was the man who scored
goals for fun in Italy's Serie A, the toughest league in the world.

"I was very close to Jimmy, very close," recalls Charles. "When I
was at Leeds I would meet up with him in Manchester. We'd have a
drink and talk about the Welsh team – who was a good player and
who was a bad player."

Murphy soon realised Charles must play in attack for Wales and
after the disappointing defeat at the hands of East Germany in
Leipzig, 'the Gentle Giant' wore the centre-forward's jersey.

Although Charles was also an excellent defender, common sense had prevailed. Wales were spoilt for choice with centre-halves but not centre-forwards.

Not all of Murphy's selections worked. In the friendly against England at Ninian Park, he tried Newcastle United's Reg Davies at inside-forward, a position Murphy was finding hard to fill.

Ironically, Wales were ripped apart that day by a player Murphy had nurtured – Duncan Edwards. Wales lost 4–0 and when England's fourth hit the back of the Welsh net, Edwards trotted over to the forlorn Murphy and said, 'Hard work Jimmy, isn't it?'

Davies, who was marking Edwards, had a poor match. Cliff Jones recalls the team-talk before this game. "Jimmy was going around all the players, telling them what to do. He went to every one – except Reg Davies. Little Reg then sticks his hand up and says, 'Boss. What should I do if Duncan Edwards is running at me with the ball?' Murphy replied, 'Reg, get out of the way – because he'll fucking kill you!'"

Two months later, and thanks to a huge slice of luck in Switzerland, Murphy was told he was just two matches away from taking part in the 1958 World Cup finals. Wales had been drawn to play Israel who were dispatched with ease.

"Qualifying for the World Cup was no less than Jimmy deserved," says Cliff Jones. "He did a tremendous job for Wales when he took over. He had a great sense of humour. I remember playing in an international against Northern Ireland at Wrexham and I went on this long run past several Irish players. Then I walked back into my own half and I was knackered.

"I heard Jimmy shouting from the bench, 'Cliff, what d'you think you're playing at! Stop standing around! Get moving!' I was about to have a go back at him when he started smiling. That was Jimmy."

For Jones, and most of his team-mates, the highlight of playing for Wales was listening to a Jimmy Murphy pep talk. "Those players who have never listened to any of Jimmy's rantings missed one of soccer's great experiences," says Jones.

"Eddie Colman told me about one of them and I've never forgotten it. It was at Old Trafford, before Munich had happened. Jimmy was giving instructions to each player, to Duncan Edwards, Dave Pegg and Eddie himself. But when he came to Billy Foulkes he just told him 'Bill, kick the fucking thing anywhere.'"

John Charles says Murphy's ability to mix in with the players earned him enormous respect.

"The admiration the players had for him was terrific. At Juventus, the manager, Ljubisa Brocic, was very strict. You couldn't drink, they didn't like it in Italy. But Jimmy would let you have a drink within reason. If there was a match in a couple of days time, he'd say 'OK lads, you can have a drink today, but tomorrow leave it alone.' He managed to be one of the lads, yet still was above us."

Ron Hewitt, the Cardiff City inside-forward and one of the new faces introduced by Murphy for the 1958 World Cup, recalls, "There were no favourites with Jimmy Murphy. It didn't matter if you played for Tottenham Hotspur or Cardiff City, everyone was treated the same. There was no favouritism. He was working at one of the biggest clubs in the country and he brought the methods they used there to the Welsh team.

"He had a couple of phrases he would always tell us in the dressing room. One of his favourites was, 'When you're out on that field remember those men working down a pit'. Another one was, 'Play for the people of Wales!' He would also say 'That lot aren't better than you! Go out and show them!' They weren't mild talks, but they were the best. After you'd heard Murphy, the team-talks back at our clubs were a bit of a let-down. We were a decent side in '58 and it was all down to Murphy. I can't praise him enough."

The United assistant manager became a wanted man after leading Wales to the quarter-finals in Sweden. Murphy was offered a huge salary to coach in Brazil and he was also approached by Arsenal. He was tempted by the job at Highbury, but in the end decided to stay with Busby at Old Trafford where together they built another great side with players such as Best, Law and Kidd. "Murphy was happy doing what he was doing," says Webster. "He could have gone anywhere but at Old Trafford Busby took the flak if results went wrong. If he became a manager Murphy would be the one who got the sack. He liked being the number two."

Murphy remained Wales manager until July 1964. He told the selectors he could no longer divide his time between Manchester and Wales, and that if he remained in charge of the national team for the 1964/65 season he would miss 14 United matches.

Results since the World Cup in Sweden had not been that impressive. Wales failed to qualify for the 1962 World Cup in Chile, losing out to Spain in qualifying, and had failed to qualify for the 1964 European Championships in Spain, having lost out to Hungary Since taking charge of Wales in October 1956 his record as manager was played 43, won 11, lost 19 and drawn 13.

The question of whether Murphy was still the right man for the job was being asked at the end of 1962. It had been Murphy's worst year as Wales manager – his team lost six out of seven matches and conceded 18 goals.

Life at Old Trafford changed for Murphy after United won the

European Cup in 1968. Busby retired as manager to become general manager and Murphy, who devoted so much of his life to the club, found himself on the periphery. United offered him early retirement and a £25 a-week scouting job which, reluctantly, he took. United never repaid the loyalty Murphy had shown them for two decades. The club decided to stop paying his taxi fares from his home to Old Trafford – Murphy did not drive – and also refused to pay his telephone bills.

Murphy carried on scouting until his death in Manchester, in 1989. He died a sad, rather than bitter, man.

CHAPTER THREE

THE BOYS OF '58

ON April 18, 1958, the selectors met in Shrewsbury to name the World Cup squad. The draw for the 1958 tournament had been made two months earlier in Zürich. Wales had been drawn in Group Three with Hungary, Mexico and Sweden.

The selectors had much to discuss. The list of candidates contained 40 names. The squad would be made up of 22 players but, to keep expenses at a minimum, only 18 would fly to Sweden and the remaining four would remain home on stand-by. Not only did the selectors have to whittle the list down to a half, but they also had to consider the stunning victory of the Wales under-23 side against England at Wrexham five days earlier. Before that match, which Wales won 2–1, several of the under-23 players would not have been in the running for Sweden. Following a tremendous display at The Racecourse, that had now changed.

There were seven automatic choices for the squad. Jack Kelsey in goal, Mel Hopkins at left-back, the captain Dave Bowen at left-half, Ivor Allchurch at inside-left, Cliff Jones at outside-left, Terry Medwin, who could play at outside-right, inside-right and even centre-forward, and above all John Charles, the Juventus centre-forward. Five of the seven, Kelsey, Allchurch, Jones, Medwin and Charles, all hailed from the Swansea area which, after the war, became one of Britain's leading football nurseries. "I think it had a lot to do with having a beach," explains Medwin. "Growing up in Swansea after the war there wasn't much to do if you were young, so most of us played football all day long on the beaches. In a way, we had our own Copacabana."

Kelsey, born in the village of Llansamlet, just outside Swansea, was not only one of the best goalkeepers in Britain, but also the world. "He was in the top three, no doubt about it," says Ken Jones, his understudy in Sweden. "Jack, in my opinion, was up there with Harry Gregg and Lev Yashin."

Kelsey left Cwm School at 14 and worked as a crane driver, a blacksmith and painter before turning to football. He joined Arsenal from local district club Winch Wen and was third-choice goalkeeper at Highbury behind George Swindin and Ted Platt. Kelsey made an unexpected debut in February 1951, against Charlton Athletic. Swindin and Platt were both injured so the 21–year-old was thrust into the action. For Kelsey, the match was a disaster as Charlton rammed five past him.

After that he disappeared into oblivion, but then resurfaced in Arsenal's championship-winning side in 1952/53 season when he established himself as Swindin's deputy. The following season, after a number of outstanding performances for The Gunners, he became Arsenal's number one. He won his first Welsh cap in March 1954, against Northern Ireland at Wrexham, in place of the injured Ron Howells. Since that day the Arsenal man was the first name on the team-sheet.

Kelsey, 28, was a chain-smoker and rarely without a cigarette in his hand. He had perfected the art of smuggling a half-smoked cigarette into the dressing room before a match. At half-time, he would nip into either the toilet or the shower, inhale a few drags and then throw the cigarette away. He was also the biggest practical joker in the Welsh team.

Arguably his finest joke was played on Mel Charles, before a match with Austria, at Wrexham in 1955. As Cliff Jones recalls, "Jack left a telegram for Mel at the hotel reception. The telegram, supposedly from a football boot firm, offered Mel £3,000 to use his name in adverts. It told Mel that representatives from the firm would meet him at the hotel that evening. We all went out that night, except Mel who sat in the hotel lobby waiting for the reps. We came back really late, it may have been close to midnight, and Mel was still sitting there, waiting. We told him the next day Jack had set him up. He hit the roof."

Ken Jones, however, saw another side to Kelsey during their stay in Sweden. "He was a mean bugger, Jack. We weren't really the best of mates. After we'd been knocked out and were going home I asked Jack if I could have one of his jerseys as a souvenir. He had about three or four. He said, 'No Ken, these are World Cup jerseys.' I kept on at him and he said he'd send me one in the post. A few weeks later this package came to me at home. It was one of Jack's old shirts, not one of the World Cup ones, and it was in a hell of a state – it looked like it was made in 1912 and he even took the badge off."

Kelsey's strengths were his positioning and clean handling. "I'd put Jack among the best three goalkeepers I've ever seen," says Cliff

Jones. "The other two were Bert Trautmann and Pat Jennings. There was only one criticism I had of Jack – he couldn't kick the ball. He was a good thrower but not a very good kicker. He never got any distance. With his right foot the ball may have reached the halfway line, but with his left foot – forget it!"

Mel Hopkins, a tall, gangly 23–year-old from the Rhondda, had made the left-back berth his own since his international debut against Northern Ireland in April 1956. Hopkins was well-established at Tottenham Hotspur, the club he joined in 1951 from Ystrad Boys Club. The fair-haired six-footer was just as useful with an oval ball as a round one, and was good enough to play rugby for the Pontypridd and District XI. But Ystrad-born Hopkins's first love was football and when, at 16, he left Tonypandy Grammar School he had no hesitation in moving to London to join Spurs. He made his league debut in 1952 when he was just 17. Deceptively quick and a strong tackler, Hopkins had matured into one of the best left-backs in British football. There was little for him to fear in Sweden, as Hopkins himself explains, "I had already played against forwards like Stanley Matthews and Tom Finney, so I was used to playing against world-class players. There was no-one harder to play against than Finney. He would beat you, cut inside and score."

During Jimmy Murphy's reign the mantle of on-the-pitch leader passed from John Charles to Dave Bowen. This was because Charles had moved to Italy, which meant he was no longer guaranteed international football since Juventus now controlled Big John's movements. However, it was easy to see why Murphy had backed 29-year-old Bowen, who was awarded the captaincy against East Germany in September 1957. The Arsenal left-half was, aside from being one of the soundest wing-halves in the game, an inspirational player. The dark-haired Bowen, much to Murphy's delight, would shout and bawl at his team-mates to drive them on. His qualities were never more evident than in Arsenal's match against Manchester United earlier that season. It was the Busby Babes's last league match before the Munich disaster. United, in front of a stunned Highbury crowd, were 3–0 up at half-time and coasting. During the interval Bowen turned on his colleagues and was responsible for the most savage dressing-down the Highbury walls had ever heard. It had an effect. In the second-half Arsenal made it 3–3 and even though they eventually lost 5–4 they had, thanks to Bowen, at least regained their dignity.

Born in Nantyffyllon, overlooking Maesteg, he left Wales when he was 15, when his parents moved to Northampton to run a pub, the Plumbers Arms. In 1948 he joined Northampton Town and two years later he was Highbury-bound after he had been spotted by Pat Whittaker, the son of the Arsenal manager Tom. Curiously, Bowen once wore the England shirt. In 1948, at Blackpool, he played for England in a boys' club international against Scotland. His Wales debut, against Yugoslavia in Cardiff in September 1954, was forgettable – Wales lost 3–1. Bowen had to wait until 1956 to become a regular and in the six matches under his captaincy, Wales had lost only once, against England in Cardiff.

Ivor Allchurch was nicknamed 'Golden Boy'. The title was apt. Not only did Allchurch have wavy blonde hair like a cherub, he was also the most naturally-gifted player in the Welsh side. Born in Swansea, the 28–year-old inside-left was considered one of Wales's few genuine world-class players. Allchurch joined the Swans in 1947 after he was spotted playing youth football, while a pupil at Plasmarl School, by Swansea scout Joe Sykes.

He made his league debut in 1949 and the following year he was playing for his country, his international debut coming in a 4–2 defeat by England at Sunderland. Allchurch had everything – flair, pace, vision, elegance, poise and, for an inside-forward, a wonderful eye for goal.

But the years leading up to the World Cup had not been happy ones for Allchurch. Because of his decision to stay in Division Two with the Swans, managers across Britain dubbed him "The Star Who Wasn't Quite" – they felt he was wasting his time, and talents, at The Vetch. In 1953, Allchurch stunned the soccer world when he turned down the chance to join Stan Cullis's mighty Wolves side. "I can't be better off anywhere else in this country," said the loyal Allchurch. "I have my friends at Swansea. I have maximum pay. I'm on full benefit." A series of leg and ankle injuries meant he missed all four qualifying matches against East Germany and Czechoslovakia, but he returned for the play-off with Israel and scored in both legs. He also looked back to his best in the friendly against Northern Ireland in Belfast, which ended 1–1, at the start of April.

Terry Medwin was arguably one of the most underrated players in the Welsh squad, overshadowed perhaps by the other Swansea-born products, Allchurch, Charles and Jones. Medwin, the son of a prison officer, was born opposite The Vetch and within a stone's throw from where his father made a living, Swansea Prison. His local club signed "the lad from the prison next door" and, fair-haired and good-looking, he soon became the Swansea Town pin-up boy, with the female supporters classing him as a cross between actors Van Johnson and Donald Houston. "I used to play football with a tennis ball at school," says Medwin. "That's how the Brazilians start." He won his first cap against Northern Ireland in April 1953, but three years later Medwin fell out with the Swans. He was being picked at centre-forward and he claimed this jeopardised his place as the outside-right in the Welsh team. Medwin demanded to play on the right-wing – if not he should be released. Swansea chose the latter and sold him to Tottenham for £18,000.

Cliff Jones came from one of Wales's most famous football families. His father, Ivor, and uncle, Bryn, both played for Wales. Jones would arrive in Sweden the most expensive winger in the British game. Tottenham had paid £35,000 for his services. At 17 'Cliffie' made his league debut for Swansea Town in a 3–1 win at Bury in October 1952. He played inside-right that day. The following year, and after a suggestion by Joe Sykes, Jones was converted to outside-left in a 2–2 draw against Stoke City. From that point, 'Cliffie' did not look back.

His first appearance for Wales was an experience the former winger would prefer to forget. It was on May 9, 1954, against Austria in Vienna. "I played really badly and we lost 2–0," he recalls. "I don't think I did one right thing. In fact, I was so bad the Welsh selectors didn't bother to watch me the next season, even though I was playing really well." Jones was given a second chance in October 1955, against England in Cardiff. This time he did himself justice. Jones not only had an excellent game, he also scored the winning goal. It was a header at the far post, a goal that would become his trademark at Tottenham and which gave the Welsh their first victory over England since 1938. "As soon as I headed it," smiles Jones, "I knew it was a goal." Jones was never dropped again.

John Charles was the one Welsh player the world feared. In most people's opinion, he remains the greatest footballer Wales has ever produced. After leaving school in 1946 he joined Swansea Town on apprentice terms, but before he could make his first senior appearance at The Vetch he was whisked off to Leeds United. Despite being more than six feet tall and weighing nearly 14 stone, Charles was as graceful as he was powerful. At Elland Road he began at centre-half but was moved to centre-forward after Jack Charlton arrived on the scene. In the 1953/54 season Big John scored a club record 42 goals as Leeds won promotion to Division One. By the end of the 1956/57 season Juventus, the Italian giants, had been alerted to Charles and they dispatched Gigi Peronace to Yorkshire to sign the man many believed was the best centre-forward, and centre-half, in the world.

The ink on Charles's contract with Juventus was only 10 days old when the selectors picked the squad for Sweden. Naturally, they placed a tick next to Charles's name, but it was a gamble. Whether 26–year-old Charles took part in the World Cup was down to Juventus. And they had not yet said yes.

That day in Shrewsbury, the selectors decided on 17 of the 18 players. The rest of the Sweden party would be Mel Charles, Stuart Williams, Derrick Sullivan, Trevor Edwards, Colin Webster, Vic Crowe, Roy Vernon, Ken Jones, Ken Leek and Colin Baker.

Mel Charles may have been in the shadow of his older brother, but the 22–year-old Swansea Town player was a good footballer in his own right. Mel, in fact, briefly joined John at Leeds but, unlike his brother, Mel was prone to homesickness and he failed to settle in Yorkshire. He broke into Swansea Town's first-team in May 1952 and won his first Welsh cap against Northern Ireland, in Belfast in 1955. Mel was the most versatile player in Murphy's pack – he looked comfortable almost anywhere on the pitch. "I played right-back, right-half, centre-half, left-half, inside-forward and centre-forward," he boasts. "Ivor (Allchurch) kept asking me why I didn't just play at centre-half, because that's where he thought I was best. But I liked going forward and scoring goals."

Murphy agreed with Allchurch. Mel's best position, as he proved against Israel, was in the heart of defence. "I'll never forget listening to the radio, waiting to hear news of the Welsh squad," smiles Charles. "I was at home in Alice Street, listening with my parents. It was 9.30pm when news of the squad came on. I've never been so nervous. I had butterflies, I was sweating, I could hear my heart beating. My name was mentioned. I think it was the fifth mentioned. After that I didn't care about anyone else!"

The burly right-back Stuart Williams, the son of a Wrexham director, partnered England international Don Howe in the West Bromwich Albion defence. Williams, born in Wrexham, signed for the Midlands club in 1950. He turned professional at The Hawthorns a year later. The selectors tended to pick players on their last performance and 27-year-old Williams, frozen out of the qualifying games, did himself no harm with two solid displays against Israel. "After the second Israel match I was very hopeful of getting into the squad," he admits. "I would've been disappointed if I hadn't been picked."

Derrick Sullivan, Cardiff City's 27-year-old auburn-haired utility player, was one of the surprise selections. At international level 'Sulli' had been out in the cold for two years. Then, in 1957, he played with distinction against Scotland and England. He missed the Israel matches but figured against Northern Ireland in Belfast, in April 1958. Like Williams, 'Sulli' – who could play right-back or right-half – appeared to have prospered from the selectors' habit of remembering players on their last display. Sullivan was one of Wales's best players against the Irish.

Born in Newport, he joined Cardiff City in 1947 but became a first-teamer after six years in the reserves. He made his international debut against Northern Ireland in 1953. 'Sulli' was one of the characters in the Welsh squad. He was laid-back, funny and, according to the players, he was also the biggest drinker. "He could drink 10–12 pints no problem," remembers his close friend and Cardiff City team-mate, Ken Jones. "Derrick and I could drink the rest of the players under the table. He introduced the lads to Aspro – after a few beers we'd put it on our tongues and it would hide the beer breath from Jimmy Murphy and the selectors."

Ken Leek, who shared a room with Sullivan during the World Cup, recalls the luggage the Cardiff City player took with him to Sweden. "He only had a small, plastic bag and he only brought two shirts with him. One of them had sailing boats all over it. He also had a shaving kit but hardly anything else so I lent him the odd shirt. He was more or less the same size as me." Williams, too, recalls Sullivan's casual attire for the World Cup campaign. "He only brought two of everything – two shirts, two pairs of trousers, two pairs of socks. He would stay, 'Stu, you can only wear one shirt at a time, one pair of socks at a time...' He was a great bloke. I remember what he was wearing on the flight to Sweden – it was a pullover which only went as far as his belly button. It looked like it belonged to a 12–year-old."

Leek, along with Ken Jones and Colin Baker, owed his place in the squad to the under-23 victory against England at Wrexham. That match was one the selectors just could not ignore. Thanks to goals from Leek and a winner from Birmingham City's Brian Orritt just two minutes from time, Wales beat an England side which featured no less than eight World Cup players as well as a young Jimmy Greaves. It was England's first ever defeat at under-23 level. "It was an excellent result and I had quite a good game," remembers Leek, who was born in Ynysybwl, near Pontypridd.

The 22–year-old inside-left, a powerful forward with an equally powerful shot, was on third division Northampton Town's books but was about to sign for Leicester City. "In the space of two months I went from Division Three to Division One to the World Cup," says Leek who was a last minute replacement for Roy Vernon in that under-23 game. "I never thought I would go to Sweden. I was playing in the third division and I was rebuilding my football career after coming out of the national service, but this match and the move to Leicester did it for me. I didn't think I'd play in the World Cup. Ivor was the inside-left and there was no way Jimmy Murphy was going to drop him. The only chance I had was if there were injuries."

The other Valleys boy who was picked following this sensational defeat of England was goalkeeper Ken Jones. The inclusion of Aberdare-born Jones, known as Jonah, raised eyebrows only because it was at the expense of Graham Vearncombe, for so long Kelsey's deputy. What made the situation more interesting was that Jones and Vearncombe were team-mates at Cardiff City. The hot-tempered Jones had already dethroned Vearncombe at Ninian Park, now he had dethroned him in the Welsh squad. "Was he cheesed off? I don't know, we never talked about it. But I would have been," admits Jones. "Graham was going through a bad patch at the time. He wasn't doing the business. It happens to us all. Trevor Morris (City's manager) said 'Well, let's take a look at this other guy' and that other guy was me. I was in the right place at the right time. It was lucky for me, unlucky for Graham."

At Ninian Park Jones was nicknamed TV Ken. It stemmed from an incident in February 1958, when City were playing Bristol Rovers. Jones arrived just five minutes before kick-off. His excuse – he had been watching an FA Cup tie between Manchester United and Fulham at home. Jones conceded two bad goals that afternoon and a furious Trevor Morris demoted him to the Welsh League team as punishment.

The 23–year-old's undoubted strength was his formidable kicking ability. Jones could kick the ball from one penalty box to the other. In the Welsh League match Morris forced him to play following the Bristol Rovers disaster, City were awarded a penalty. Jones decided he would take it. He hit the ball so hard it burst. "I knew with Jack around I wasn't going to play in the World Cup," says Jones, "but I knew it would be a hell of an experience."

Colin Baker joined Cardiff City on amateur terms in 1950 from Cardiff Nomads. Born in the Tremorfa area of the city, Baker, shy and unassuming, replaced his namesake Billy Baker at left-half although he could play at right-half as well. "I was surprised to be included, especially when you consider defenders of the calibre of Alan Harrington and Ray Daniel were left out. I had never played for Wales before and the England game was my first under-23. I was delighted just to be a part of it all." Baker, who was 23 at the time of the 1958 World Cup, adds, "I had a fair game against England, but the call-up still came out of the blue." Baker also helped his cause when, two days before the selectors met in Shrewsbury, he scored in City's 3–0 win over Fulham at Ninian Park.

The selectors also placed a tick next to Manchester United's Colin

Webster. Without doubt Murphy, who had taken over the reigns at Old Trafford post-Munich, had some influence on Webster's selection. The 25–year-old centre-forward played the first qualifier against Czechoslovakia, but, after a mediocre 90 minutes, Cardiff-born Webster vanished without trace. He was dropped for the two matches behind the Iron Curtain, the home match against East Germany, the friendlies against England and Scotland, the two Israel matches and the World Cup warm-up against Northern Ireland. But Webster was now one of the lucky 18. "Murphy picked me because he knew what I could do," recalls Webster.

Webster joined United after being given a free-transfer by Cardiff City in 1952. "Do you know why they got rid of me at Cardiff? Because Bob John (the trainer) thought I was an alcoholic! I was doing my national service up in Catterick and I was going down to Bournemouth on the train because City were playing there. On the train I got chatting to somebody and before I got off he gave me a bottle of beer. I didn't drink so I gave the beer to Charlie Rutter, one of the other players. This was in the hotel foyer in Bournemouth and Bob John saw me. He then had me down as an alcoholic and that was the end of me and Cardiff."

He was snapped up by United but, because of the fierce competition for places, first-team appearances were limited. Webster would have been on the plane that crashed in Munich, but a bout of flu may have saved his life. "It was the day before the team flew to Belgrade. We had just played Arsenal and I was the twelfth man. We were staying in a hotel in London and I had a slight flu. Busby ordered me home. He didn't want me around the other players if I was ill. Personally, I thought I was fit to travel, but I got into a taxi and came back to Manchester." A few days later most of his team-mates, and friends, were dead. Webster was in bed with a temperature of 102 when news of the crash filtered through. "I often think I could have died on the runway," says Webster. "I was lucky. For me, it wasn't to be."

In the Munich aftermath Webster, no longer a reserve, became a key man for United. The Cardiffian with a sallow complexion scored the winning goal against West Brom in the FA Cup quarter-final. The other side of Webster was seen in the final itself. After a fierce tackle on Bolton's inside-forward, Dennis Stevens, a 22–man brawl nearly broke out on the Wembley turf. This was the risk of playing the fiery Webster in Sweden. How would the other teams, and above all the referees, react to his aggressive tackling? Wales already had little chance of winning with 11 men on the field. They could ill-afford being reduced to 10.

After scoring the winning goal against Czechoslovakia in May 1957, it was fitting that Roy Vernon should be selected. Born in Ffynnongroew, near Holywell in North Wales, 21-year-old Vernon was already a star at Blackburn Rovers where his pace and brilliant dribbling skills enthralled Ewood Park. After playing for Welsh YMCA and Mostyn YMCA, Vernon joined Blackburn in 1955 and won his first cap against Northern Ireland in April 1957 – a year ahead of schedule. He also played in the 4–1 win against East Germany and in the matches against England and Scotland.

Trevor Edwards, Charlton Athletic's 21–year-old right-back, had won his seat on the flight to Stockholm despite a torrid performance in Leipzig against East Germany nearly a year earlier. Edwards, born in Penygraig, in the Rhondda, joined the London club in 1955 and won his first cap in 1957, against Northern Ireland. He looked doubtful for the World Cup party after his East German nightmare, but after a fine performance in the under-23 match against England he won over the selectors.

Vic Crowe was the Welshman with the Brummie accent. His family moved to Birmingham when he was two and Crowe was signed by West Brom as an amateur. After finishing his national service the Abercynon-born left-half was spotted by Aston Villa's scouts and soon he was on his way to Villa Park. He would have played in Villa's 1957 FA Cup-winning team but, because of a knee injury, he lost his place to Stan Crowther. He regained his shirt during the 1957/58 season and played so well that Villa sold Crowther to Manchester United. Crowe, 25, had yet to play for Wales and with Bowen at left-half there was little chance of a debut in Sweden.

The selectors failed to agree on who would be the eighteenth man. It was a toss-up between Manchester United winger Ken Morgans, a survivor of the Munich crash, and Cardiff City's inside-right Ron Hewitt. Three days later, on May 1, the selectors plumped for Hewitt. They had planned to watch Morgans in the FA Cup final but when Murphy announced 18–year-old Morgans was not physically or mentally fit to play, the last seat on the plane went to 29-year-old Hewitt. "I think I would have gone to Sweden. Jimmy told me before the disaster that he was going to take me," recalls Morgans, a promising outside-right. "In fact, he told me before the Arsenal game, which was just a few days before the Munich tragedy, that I would be part of the Welsh squad."

At 18, Morgans was the youngest of the Busby Babes. He was the last to be pulled from the wreck of the Elizabethan airliner that cold February afternoon in Munich. Buried under piles of luggage in the cargo hold, the Swansea teenager was spotted by a keen-eyed

German reporter who was searching through the twisted metal. Doctors recommended he should take a year off football, but seven weeks later, because of the chronic shortage of first-team players, Morgans was back playing for United. "I felt dreadful. I'd lost a lot of weight. I'd gone from 11 stone to nine stone. I wasn't fit, but because there weren't enough players I had to play," he explains. "I lost that couple of yards pace. I just lost it. I was very quick. A full-back could have five yards on me and I'd still beat him. But after Munich I couldn't do that anymore. In a way, I wasn't surprised to be left out of the World Cup squad." Although he survived the crash he was never the same player. Morgans, now 59 and who lives in Swansea, stayed at Old Trafford until 1961 before ending an unfulfilled career with Swansea Town and Newport County. He ran a pub in Pontypool and worked as a rep for a tool business and then a shipping agency before retiring in 1997. He never played for his country at senior level. "I'm sure the crash took it out of me. I had headaches for a couple of years. I used to have nightmares about the crash and the players who were killed."

Ron Hewitt moved to Cardiff from Wrexham in 1957, claiming a move south was the only way to get international recognition. "I scored a lot of goals at Cardiff, a lot of winning goals as well. If you played for Cardiff there was a good chance you'd get picked for Wales because nearly all the selectors were down in South Wales," says Hewitt, a clever inside-right.

He played well against Israel in Cardiff but badly against Northern Ireland two months later and the selectors, who thought they had unearthed a new star, had second thoughts. However, Morgans's poor fitness swung in Hewitt's favour.

Flint-born Hewitt, one of 13 children, was signed by Wolves manager Stan Cullis in 1948. "He was a bastard but a good bastard. I learnt all my good habits from Cullis. No smoking, no drinking and in bed by 9pm. If you broke any of his rules he'd fine you a week's wages," says Hewitt, who drank only orange juice as a player. At Molineux he played in the reserves and was loaned to Walsall, then Darlington. In 1950 he was sold to Wrexham and finished top scorer in his first year with 16 goals. "When I was selected for the World Cup a telegram came for me at Ninian Park," he smiles. "It said, 'Congratulations. Mr Cullis'."

On the day Hewitt was confirmed, the selectors also decided on the four stand-by players. They were Cardiff City goalkeeper Graham Vearncombe, Ipswich Town wing-half John Elsworthy, Swansea Town outside-right Len Allchurch and Plymouth Argyle striker George Baker. Nantyderry-born Elsworthy had never been capped while Penrhiwceiber-born Baker's last outing for Wales was in 1948, against Northern Ireland. Out of the four, Allchurch and Vearncombe figured in the qualifying matches. These four would remain in Britain during the competition, and would be flown over to Sweden only if they were needed. Cardiff-born Vearncombe died of a heart attack in 1993, aged 59. Allchurch, now 65, lives in Swansea.

There was heartbreak for several players. Ron Stitfall, Dai Thomas, Bill Harris, Alan Harrington and Des Palmer had all featured in qualifying matches but found themselves excluded from the 22–man squad. "Jimmy Murphy wanted me to play a retreating game. That was his style," says 73-year-old Stitfall, now Wales's kit manager after years of installing heaters. "But at Cardiff I got the ball to the winger as quickly as possible. That was my style. What Jimmy wanted was foreign to my natural game, but he never told me why he dropped me which is disappointing. If a manager explains something there is a better chance the player will understand. What Jimmy did happens in football."

Stitfall's team-mate, Harrington, dislocated his shoulder six months earlier in a match against Manchester City. Unluckily, the injury returned when the selectors were studying his form. He recalls, "I missed the last league match before the squad was picked (against Fulham at Ninian Park on April 26). I had been playing with a harness on my right shoulder but it was really uncomfortable and every time I was in a heavy challenge my shoulder would pop out." Harrington, now 65, works part-time as a purchasing manager for a chemical company in Cardiff. "It was a toss-up between myself and Colin Baker, and Colin got it. When the tournament was going on I had an operation on my shoulder. I was in hospital for eight days."

Des Palmer looked a certain bet for the squad after scoring a hat-trick against the East Germans at Ninian Park, but a thigh injury ended his World Cup dream. It happened against England, on October 19, 1957, at Ninian Park. In the first couple of minutes Palmer tried to sprint past the great Billy Wright. "I felt a rip in my right leg behind my knee right up to my backside," recalls 67-year-old Palmer, another Swansea-born player. "It was a terrible feeling. My muscle had gone. Because there were no subs I had to carry on and I think that match killed my career." Palmer hobbled for the remaining 88 minutes and was a bystander as England thrashed Wales 4–0. "I would have loved to have gone to Sweden. It was a once-in-a-lifetime opportunity. I still think of what could have been."

Injuries devastated Palmer's career. He joined Liverpool in 1959 but suffered an injury to his right knee in his very first game, against Leeds, and needed a double cartilage operation. Palmer's glittering future at Anfield lasted 90 minutes. "I got injured just after half-time," he recalls. "In those days there were no subs so you had to play on. Of course, that made the injury worse." He ended his career in South Africa and Australia, coached abroad for the British Council then worked for an insurance company for 15 years before retiring in 1990. "I was very unlucky with injuries at crucial times. I felt I would have gone to Sweden. It was my time to do well."

Dai Thomas, now 72, worked for Port Talbot Borough Council after hanging up his boots. He lives in Neath. Harris worked as an insurance agent in Middlesbrough after quitting the game. He died in 1989, aged 61.

Ray Daniel, Trevor Ford and Derek Tapscott are considered three of Wales's finest post-war footballers. But, for a variety of reasons, the Welsh FA considered them personae non gratae. The high-minded selectors had decided there was no way Daniel, Ford and Tapscott, despite their undoubted talents, would fly to Sweden.

Daniel, 29, one of the classiest defenders in British football, saw his international career come to an end after the 2–0 defeat against Czechoslovakia in Prague. In this match Daniel had scored an own-goal, but this was not the reason he was banished. On the team coach, as the Welsh party were returning to their hotel after the game, Daniel incurred the wrath of Herbert Powell, the Welsh FA's religious secretary. As journalist Jim Hill recalls, "Ray was sitting at the back of the bus and he started singing out loud songs from the musical *Guys and Dolls* – 'When you see a guy reach for stars in the sky, you can bet he was doing it for some doll' (Cliff Jones described the song as "a bluish number").

"This was typical of Ray who was a pretty brash guy, but it offended Powell who was a member of the Church in Wales and who liked to sing hymns during a journey," says Hill. "Whether he felt Ray should have been miserable after the defeat instead of singing songs, I don't know. But Powell got up from his seat, walked to the back of the bus and had a quiet word with Ray." Daniel, who was 29 when the World Cup squad was named, never again played for his country. "Most of the committee men were churchgoers," adds Medwin, "and they didn't like Ray singing what they considered dirty songs."

Hill recalls another incident which demonstrated bachelor Powell's prudery. During the trip to the bleak East German city of Leipzig, before Wales faced East Germany in a World Cup qualifier, Powell was taken on a shopping trip by one of the interpreters. He wanted to buy a present for his sister, Violet, who he doted on. Powell, after touring Leipzig's streets, returned to the hotel empty-handed. According to Hill, the interpreter had spotted a sculpture of a bull and recommended Powell should buy it. "I couldn't possibly buy it," said Powell, after returning to the hotel, "because its penis was exposed."

Daniel later joined Cardiff City and Swansea Town, and became player-manager of Hereford United. He ran a post office in his native Swansea until his retirement in 1989, then he moved to Clevedon. Daniel died in November 1997, aged 69.

For decades, Derek Tapscott, when asked why he missed the World Cup, said it was because of injury to his right knee. Now, 40 years on, 'Tappy' reveals the truth. "Cardiff City wanted to buy me," says Barry-born Tapscott who was an Arsenal player at the time. "One of the Welsh selectors came to watch me at Highbury and after the game he came to see me in the directors' lounge. He said if I signed for Cardiff I would go to the World Cup in Sweden." The selector was the late Fred Dewey, a Cardiff City director. "He thought he could get me on that type of sting, but I wouldn't be blackmailed. I said 'No thank you, I'm staying at Arsenal' and I walked away. A player is supposed to be in the squad on ability, not whether he signs for a club or not."

Tapscott, then 25, was not picked for World Cup duty. He made two more appearances for Wales, against England and Northern Ireland, in 1959. In his five years at Highbury, 'Tappy' – who could play inside-right or centre-forward – scored 61 goals in 119 appearances. Ironically, he joined Cardiff City in the September after the World Cup. "My father was ill so I came back home," says Tapscott. "I've never before said what happened to me in 1958. I've lived with it all my life. I'm not a yes-man and I paid for it then. Jimmy Murphy had a big say in who was in the team, but at the end of the day it was up to the selectors. We could have gone all the way to the final if a forward like myself or Trevor (Ford) was playing, but the selectors left some of the best players behind."

Today, Tapscott is a self-employed sales representative, touring South Wales selling rugby and football gear. "I would say the squad for Sweden was 70 per cent right, not 100 per cent. They should have taken me, Ray Daniel, Trevor Ford and maybe Alf Sherwood (full-back) as well. Alf had a lot of experience and was still playing well for Newport County. I was having problems with my knee that season but before the World Cup, I was fit."

In 1956, Trevor Ford's autobiography, *I Lead The Attack*, was published. It caused a sensation, exposing the illegal payments made by his former club, Sunderland, to their players, including Ford himself. The Swansea-born striker, famous for charging goalkeepers, admitted accepting £100 "under-the-counter" to join Sunderland from Aston Villa. The FA came down hard on 'Terrible Trevor' who was with Cardiff City when the book hit the shops. Ford was banned from league football for three seasons and went into exile in Holland, where he played, with considerable success, for PSV Eindhoven.

Technically, he could have still played for Wales but not surprisingly the selectors would have nothing to do with a player who admitted accepting illegal payments. Ford's last game for his country was the 2–2 draw against Scotland in Cardiff, in October 1956. After the first World Cup qualifier against Czechoslovakia, when the lack of cover at centre-forward was exposed, there were rumours that Ford would be picked for his country. They were swiftly scotched. "There is no question of such a thing happening," insisted Milwyn Jenkins, chairman of the Welsh FA. "The suggestion is sheer nonsense. The position is such that we would not dream of playing him." Ford's international career was finished. When, on April 28, the selectors discussed the squad for the 1958 World Cup, his name was never mentioned.

"I regret what happened," says Ford, "because I could have done something in Sweden. I would have been useful to Wales. I don't know why the book caused such an uproar. What happened to me was unfair because I was only being honest. When I wrote the book I didn't think we would qualify. When we did, I was sick. I was crying my eyes out in Holland."

There were few strikers in British football as prolific as Ford – at Aston Villa he scored 59 goals in 121 appearances, at Sunderland it was 67 in 108 and at Cardiff City, 39 in 69. In 1958, even though he was 34, Ford still knew where the goal was. He had just scored an incredible 51 goals for PSV during the 1957/58 season. Ford, after 30 years working in the motor industry, took a job in financial management in 1990. A keep-fit fanatic, he retired in 1994 and lives in Swansea.

"I would have done well in Sweden. Put it this way, the opposition would have known I was playing." says Ford, now 75. "I was a shoulder-charger, I could head the ball. I hadn't lost anything. I still had a lot to offer. PSV played clubs in Spain, Italy and Germany and I was scoring against all of them. If I'd known Wales would qualify I wouldn't have written the book. I would have written it afterwards."

By ignoring Ford, the selectors made a mistake. With Tapscott out and Palmer injured, the Welsh squad which arrived in Stockholm was alarmingly short of centre-forwards. It would cost Wales dear. In the quarter-final against Brazil, there would be no John Charles, kicked to pieces by Hungary in the first-round play-off. The only replacement was little Colin Webster who, that afternoon in Gothenburg, rarely troubled the Brazilian defence. How Nilton Santos and his colleagues, in particular goalkeeper Gilmar, would have coped with 'Terrible Trevor' no-one will ever know.

CHAPTER FOUR

THE WORLD'S MOST VALUABLE PLAYER

JUNE 2, 1958. The day the Welsh party left for Sweden. At London Airport they boarded BEA Flight 210, scheduled to leave for Stockholm at 9.05am. One by one they took their seats – Jimmy Murphy, the manager, Jack Jones, the trainer, William Hughes, the doctor, Milwyn Jenkins, chairman of the Welsh FA, Herbert Powell, secretary of the Welsh FA, and his sister Violet. Then there were the 11 selectors, three of whom had brought their wives, and five Welsh FA councillors.

The players – Bowen, Allchurch, Medwin, Kelsey, Sullivan, Hopkins, Webster and the rest – sat together on the plane. But John Charles, who had just completed a hugely successful first season with Juventus in Italy, was conspicuous by his absence. Juventus had finally agreed to release him but with less than a week before the opening match against the Hungarians, Charles had not been given clearance by the Italian Football Federation to play in Sweden.

For Murphy and the Welsh selectors the loss of Charles would be a fatal blow to the country's wafer-thin World Cup hopes. The Welsh side contained other quality players such as Cliff Jones, Medwin and of course 'Golden Boy' Allchurch. But it also contained several who were no more than bread-and-butter club players, some of whom played for Cardiff City and Swansea Town in Division Two.

Charles was a world star who could make the difference between victory and defeat. In his first season in Italy the Swansea-born forward had been a sensation. He finished as Serie A 'capocannoniere' (top scorer) with 28 goals as Juventus won the championship for the first time in six years.

He was signed by the Turin giants from Leeds in 1957 for £67,000, a record for a British player. Nearly a year on and Juventus now valued the man they called 'il Buono Gigante' (the Gentle Giant) at £150,000 which made him the world's most valuable footballer.

The Juventus striker was the key to Murphy's basic but effective game plan. Medwin and Jones, the two wingers, were told to get as many crosses in as possible. Hopefully, Charles, who had no peers in the air, would be on the end of one or two of them.

As the plane flew over the Baltic Sea towards the Swedish capital, Murphy was anxious. He might have to play the World Cup without his greatest asset. Who, if Charles was not there, was going to score the goals?

The John Charles dilemma had started on the evening of April 18, 1957, in the Queens Hotel in Leeds, when 'The Gentle Giant' signed a two-year contract for Juventus. As Charles, after several hours of negotiations, signed his name on the dotted line he instantly became a wealthy man. Juventus would pay him a £10,000 signing-on fee, an impressive monthly salary plus bonuses. In Italy, there was no such thing as a maximum wage. For footballers like Charles, the sky was the limit.

In signing the contract Charles became Britain's richest footballer but he also placed his international career in the hands of Juventus.

In 1958, the rules regarding club and country were simple. The selectors could call players for national team duty if they were registered with their national association. Even when Charles was at Leeds United there was no guarantee he would be released for Wales. He was a Welsh player registered with the English FA, but there were few examples of an English club refusing to let Welsh, Scottish or Irish players appear for their country.

In Italy, it was different. Internationals were usually held on a Saturday while Serie A games were played on Sunday which meant there was little chance of Juventus president Umberto Agnelli releasing Charles.

"I lost quite a few caps playing in Italy," admits Charles. "Juventus wouldn't always let me go. If they were playing just before or just after an international I would have to stay behind. It broke my heart.

"You can win championships and cups but there's no feeling like playing for your country. I loved playing for Wales. It meant a lot to me."

Charles made his international debut at the age of 18, against Northern Ireland in a World Cup qualifier at Wrexham. Charles played at centre-half, the role he played for his club Leeds United. It was hardly the best of debuts. Charles, besieged by nerves, had to mark Aston Villa's Dave Walsh. The match ended 0–0 but Walsh ran the teenager ragged. The distraught Charles was convinced his international career was over.

Just over a year later, he was given a second chance. The opponents were Switzerland. The venue, much to Charles's chagrin, was Wrexham. Wales won 3–2 but Charles, again at centre-half, had not played well. His third chance came after England crushed Wales 5–2 at Wembley in November 1952.

Not surprisingly, heads rolled and for the next international, against Northern Ireland in Belfast five months later. Charles was back, this time as inside-right.

By now Leeds had converted him, with considerable success, to centre-forward. For Wales, that position was held by Trevor Ford so Charles replaced Newcastle United's Reg Davies.

Wales won 3–2 and the day belonged to Charles. He scored the first two goals and laid on the third for Ford. From then on Charles's name was on every Welsh team-sheet – until 1957 when he went to Italy. In his contract with Juventus there was no clause allowing Charles to play for Wales whenever there was an international match.

"To be honest I didn't think we'd qualify for the World Cup," he now admits. "The World Cup was completely out of my mind. I thought the problem would never arise.

"The agents didn't bother about whether I should play for my country. This thing of club and country hadn't come around yet. I don't think agents were experienced about this matter and it was only after cases like mine that players and agents sat up and took notice of this problem."

Murphy and the selectors were forced to sweat over their star player throughout the qualifying games. Every international Charles played after April 1957 was potentially his last.

"You've got to look at it from Juventus's point of view," says Charles. "They'd paid a lot of money for me and they were worried to death I'd get injured.

"They were paying my wages so I had to do what they told me. I didn't have the privilege of saying what I could or couldn't do. Sometimes they'd let me go, other times they wouldn't. If it was an important match, they tended to let me go. That wasn't always the case with friendlies."

Charles was given the nod to play in the first World Cup qualifier against Czechoslovakia in Cardiff as well as the two away matches behind the Iron Curtain, in Leipzig and Prague.

Later in the year, the disputes started. Agnelli, whose family ran the giant motor vehicle company FIAT, blocked Charles playing in the final qualifier against East Germany in Cardiff, in September. Wales had by then lost to both Czechoslovakia and East Germany and were out of the running for a World Cup place. The Welsh forward was told the match was not important enough for him to be put at risk. For good measure, Charles was also refused leave to play against England in October and Scotland in November.

"Unfortunately we have so many new players in our side that they have not yet knitted together and it is essential they have plenty of practice before meeting the stronger clubs in the league," announced Agnelli.

He added Juventus would do its best to release Charles for internationals, but not when it conflicted with the club's interests.

"John is fighting hard for us," said Agnelli, "and we want to show that we can do the decent thing by him."

For the two vital matches with Israel, in January and February 1958, Agnelli gave his blessing for Charles to join his compatriots, but after the first game in Tel Aviv the issue raised its head once again. Charles picked up a small injury in Israel but played in Juventus's next match at Roma. Charles was anonymous and Juventus crashed 4–1. A furious Agnelli blamed the Israel match for Charles's lacklustre performance and rumours started that the club was considering a ban on Charles playing for Wales. A fortnight later, he was in Cardiff for the second match but Juventus took the hard-line approach in April, when Wales were scheduled to meet Northern Ireland in a friendly. Charles was told, 'You are going nowhere!' Agnelli insisted he play in an Italian Cup match on April 22 – the day of the international in Belfast. For the first time since he arrived in Turin, Charles publicly hit back at his employers. "They've told me I can't play and I'm far from happy about it," he said at the time. "I've never felt so down in the dumps. We lost 1–0 yesterday. Maybe if we'd won it would have been different."

Charles had a point. Juventus's bans usually coincided with a defeat.

Far worse was to follow for Charles. Since Italy, beaten by Northern Ireland, would not be travelling to Sweden, the Federcalcio – the Italian FA – decided to play Italian Cup matches in June and July. This meant Juventus could decide to retain the services of 'il Buono Gigante' during the 1958 World Cup. Charles says when he asked Agnelli if he could play in Sweden, Agnelli refused and so began a long, drawn-out fiasco which was only resolved on June 4, five days before the Hungary match.

"I thought they would let me go to Sweden but they said no," he recalls. "The Italian Cup was not an important competition. It was a run-out for the reserves."

The Italian FA said the best players were needed to ensure the competition was a success, but was Charles really needed for these games? The three sides Juventus had to face in the Italian Cup were Biella, Verneli and Torino. Biella and Verneli were two small, provincial clubs and a reserve Juventus side would make sure their 12,000-capacity stadiums sold out. As for Torino, they were Juventus's city rivals and the Turin derby guaranteed a full house.

"I was top scorer that year with 28 goals. That's a lot in Italian football but it made it harder for Juventus to release me," explains Charles.

It was easy to see why Juventus were so protective – and possessive – of their new signing. In the three years before Charles arrived, La Vecchia Signora (the Grand Old Lady, as the club are affectionately known in Italy) finished seventh, ninth and ninth again. But in Charles's first season they were crowned champions for the tenth time in their history, eight points ahead of second-placed Fiorentina.

Charles was confident his employers would let him participate in the World Cup since Juventus had clinched the championship on May 4, more than a month before Wales's first match. But along came the Italian Cup.

What had made Charles's position even more galling was that five Swedish players in Italy – Liedholm with Milan, Hamrin with Padova, Skoglund with Inter, Selmosson with Lazio and Gustavsson with Atalanta – had all been released to play in the World Cup.

"I remember thinking, 'Why can they play and not me?' Different clubs had different rules and at Juventus we were always challenging for something so the club wanted to keep its best players," says Charles.

But on April 24, Juventus announced that Charles would be released to play in Sweden. "Charles fully deserves the honour of playing for his country," said Agnelli. Asked why the sudden change of heart, the Italians refused to comment, although the word in Turin was that the World Cup release was a "thank you" present because Charles had done so well in his first season.

However, Charles tells a slightly different story. "Agnelli gave me his word of honour that if Wales beat Israel I could play for them in the World Cup. When I reminded him of his promise he said I could go.

"I would have been annoyed with Juventus if they didn't support me. I wouldn't have walked out on them but I would have been moody for the rest of my time there. It was in their interests to keep me happy."

Charles, though, had not yet won. Before he and his wife Peggy could celebrate Charles was given bleak news. The Italian FA said Charles could not travel to Sweden because insufficient notice had been given for his release. The striker was still grounded but Agnelli said he would plead to the Federcalcio on his behalf.

Charles waited anxiously for the Federcalcio's final decision at his palatial home in the hills overlooking Turin. Meanwhile, the Welsh party arrived at their base, the Grand Hotel in Soltsjöbaden, minus their star attraction. The Swedish organisers, who were relying on Charles to add a few thousand to every gate, were horrified.

There were genuine fears the sixth World Cup would be a flop. Ticket sales had been lukewarm. The German FA had returned 19,000 unsold tickets. At Västeras, only 18,000 of the 42,000 tickets printed for the Scotland-Yugoslavia match had been sold.

The only sell-outs were the three first-round matches involving Brazil. Not even Sweden's games had sold out. The organisers wanted as many of the world's top footballers to appear in Sweden. Charles was one of them.

Already four of football's great names would be absent from the competition. Stanley Matthews, at 43, was considered too old and was not included in the England squad; Ferenc Puskas, who had defected to the west during the Hungarian Uprising, could no longer play for Hungary; Alfredo di Stefano, the Real Madrid genius, played for Spain and they had not qualified; Omar Sivori lost his right to play for Argentina after joining Juventus and Juan Schiaffino, Uruguay's hero in 1950, had been 'nationalised' by Italy, who had failed to qualify. The 1958 tournament was in danger of losing yet another superstar, John Charles.

The Welsh selectors had booked a room for Charles in the Grand Hotel but they were now pessimistic. As each day passed there was no sign of the Italian FA reversing its decision. Murphy cut a particularly unhappy figure in the hotel's foyer. "How can I stage proper rehearsals without knowing whether he (Charles) will turn out or not?" he snapped.

Without Big John the players feared the worst. "If John didn't play the other teams would have been more relaxed playing against us," says Hewitt. "If we were to have a chance we needed John. We had two wingers, Terry and Cliff, but without John our system was useless. But Jimmy still kept on saying we could do it without John."

Charles's brother, Mel, says, "Without John we didn't have a chance of reaching the quarter-finals. He was such an important player for us."

With the Hungary match 96 hours away Charles, and Wales, were finally put out of their misery. The Italian FA announced it would allow Charles to travel to Sweden if Juventus and their three Italian Cup opponents agreed to his absence. They all did.

"I was beginning to feel very downhearted. It was a relief when I was told I could go. I mean, how many times does a player get to play in the World Cup?" says Charles. That morning, in the sunshine, he trained for an hour in the Stadio Comunale, the stadium where Juventus played. In the afternoon, he caught a plane to Sweden, via Copenhagen. He arrived at Bromma Airport, in Stockholm, at 3am on June 5. The plane was due to arrive at around 11pm but was delayed in Copenhagen after it developed mechanical trouble. The striker, on arrival at Bromma, found there was nobody from the Welsh FA to welcome him.

"No-one was there, as usual!" quips Charles. "I don't think they knew I was coming." In fact, one of the selectors, Fred Dewey, had travelled to Bromma to meet Charles but he left shortly after midnight. He returned to the Grand Hotel, resigned to the fact Wales would have to make do without Big John.

"The airport was practically empty when I arrived," remembers Charles. "But I was a big lad, I could look after myself. I spent an hour-and-a-half trying to find where the Welsh team were staying. I was getting ready to sleep in the airport. I would have slept on one of the seats until the morning."

He was rescued by his friend, Dewi Lewis, the *Western Mail* football correspondent, who drove Charles to nearby Soltsjöbaden. The Swedish newspapers, which had covered the Charles-Juventus story religiously, later claimed the Welsh FA officials ignored its star player when he arrived in Stockholm in the early hours.

"They were lovely people, the selectors," says Charles, "but they were ordinary people and they were inexperienced when it came to going abroad." He is the only surviving member of the squad to say anything kind about the 16 officials.

If Charles was expecting a lie-in later that morning he was in for a shock. "Jimmy got me out of bed for training. I had to train with all the other players, and you did what the master says."

At breakfast Charles walked into the hotel dining room to a rapturous, almost surreal, reception. As his brother Mel recalls, "I'll never forget it. John walked in. He looked like a Greek god because he was so tall and bronzed. The selectors saw him, threw down their knives and forks, stood up and started singing 'For he's a jolly good fellow, for he's a jolly good fellow..' It was like a kids' party." Earlier in the morning they had left him stranded at the airport in Stockholm. Now they were singing his name.

The man himself remembers that morning well. "I walked in, sat down, then all of a sudden the selectors started singing – the wives as well! Usually they were very quiet, they didn't say a word and here they were singing at me with Jimmy conducting them. I was very embarrassed. All the players were laughing their heads off."

After breakfast, outside the hotel, Charles was surrounded by cameras and reporters all wanting a piece of the Juventus superstar. He then trained with the rest of his colleagues at the local sports ground.

The presence of the Juventus striker was a massive boost to the rest of the squad. "Now we felt we had a chance," says Hewitt. "John was the player they all feared."

During breakfast, Derrick Sullivan approached the sleepy-eyed Charles and said, "John, you're the greatest thing that's arrived in Soltsjöbaden since sliced bread." After a typically gruelling Murphy training session Charles returned to his hotel room and slept off the previous night's trip.

Wales and the World Cup organisers were relieved. Without Charles, the Welsh would not have been an attractive draw for the neutrals. After his arrival, the Swedish press criticised Juventus for their handling of the Charles affair. A Stockholm paper, *Aftonbladet*, was scathing. It claimed, despite Agnelli's very public support for Charles, that Juventus were behind the Italian FA's ban.

"They played him a dirty, under-handed trick and it is good to know that he has stood up to them and got his way. It was clear that Juventus first of all gave him permission to travel, but then went behind his back and got the Italian FA to ban him from the World Cup competition."

Strong words, so strong in fact that Charles was forced to issue a public statement defending Agnelli and Juventus the day after the newspaper's allegations were printed. Charles described Agnelli as "a man of his word" and added, "Signor Agnelli, to my personal knowledge, intervened on my behalf and the Italian FA immediately raised the ban on my playing in the World Cup."

Aftonbladet did not stop with the Italians. It also blamed the Welsh FA for not resolving the matter sooner. The newspaper attacked the Welsh FA for sending letters to Juventus asking for Charles's release and said that officials should have flown to Turin to discuss the situation. The latter method, it said, had worked for the

Swedes when discussing releases for Liedholm, Hamrin, Skoglund, Selmosson and Gustavsson.

"Sweden sent their most influential football man to Italy," continued *Aftonbladet*, "despite the fact he had a thousand important jobs to do at home, and he succeeded in getting the release of Swedish players without undue difficulty. How can the FA of Wales expect to get Charles released by letter only?"

Charles remained in Italy for another four years, until 1962. The five years in Turin, he says, were among the five happiest years of his life but the club-country dilemma was one of the reasons he returned to Britain with Leeds United, the club where he made his name. After the 1958 World Cup, the problem of getting released for Wales remained. Charles found it even harder to gain permission.

"I enjoyed playing for Wales because it also gave me a break from Italian football," he explains. "It was nice to have a change, to play for another team."

Before he left for Stockholm, Agnelli had warned him the World Cup matches would be his last for Wales for some time. When Charles returned to Turin he discovered Agnelli had not changed his mind. From September 1958 to October 1961 the centre-forward missed 20 games for Wales. By 1961 Charles had had enough. His contract was up that year. The Italians had refused him permission to play in the two vital World Cup qualifiers against Spain, in Cardiff and Madrid.

When Charles told Agnelli he was returning to Britain the club president offered him a king's ransom to stay. If he re-signed with Juventus he would receive £18,000 – which included the then staggering amount of £14,000 as a signing-on fee – in one year alone. But the Welshman turned it down and, for the second time in his life, he signed for Leeds.

Ironically, the situation did not improve in England. With the European Championship qualifier with Hungary in Budapest looming in December, Leeds told Charles they would not release him because they wanted him to play in a friendly against his old club Juventus.

His return to Yorkshire was as brief as it was unhappy. At the end of November he agreed a return to Italy, this time with Roma. Charles had learned his lesson. His contract contained one condition, that he would be released to play in Wales's matches. "I wouldn't have left Britain," he says, "if I hadn't had this guarantee in my contract."

CHAPTER FIVE

WELCOME TO SOLTSJÖBADEN

BEFORE flying to Stockholm the Welsh squad assembled in London for five days. For the last fortnight the players, by order of the Welsh FA, had been told to rest "preferably by the sea" following a gruelling nine-month league season. Now Murphy had to get his 18 players tuned, both physically and mentally, for the World Cup and London was the first step.

They stayed in the Lancaster Court Hotel, directly opposite Hyde Park and a quick walk from the Football Association's headquarters at Lancaster Gate. Wales were not the only World Cup team using the hotel. They were joined by England who were using the Lancaster Court as their last stop before jetting off to Sweden.

In London, Wales's alarming lack of preparation came to light. During the qualifying rounds the Welsh had shown their amateurism by taking a pitiful squad of 13 players behind the Iron Curtain to play East Germany and Czechoslovakia in a week. Now, hours after arriving at the Lancaster Court, Murphy's patience was well and truly put to the test.

First, and most embarrassingly of all, Derrick Sullivan had forgotten his passport. The stunned Murphy had to send a telegram to his home in Newport asking his wife, Sheila, to send her husband's passport to the Lancaster Court Hotel. "Derrick felt really daft," recalls his Cardiff City team-mate, Ron Hewitt. "He was in a bit of a panic saying, 'How the hell did I forget it?' But Jimmy was calm about it. He told Sulli, 'Don't worry we'll get it!' I think Derrick was so concerned about playing in Sweden that he forgot something like his passport. Don't forget, we only played for Cardiff City and we hardly needed our passports playing for them."

Terry Medwin adds, "If I was told one of the lads had forgotten his passport I would have guessed it was Derrick. He was such a care-free character. It was lucky we were in London for a few days because it gave him time to get his passport. Otherwise, he would have had to have stayed behind or catch a later flight to Sweden – that's if the Welsh FA decided to pay for him a second time."

Aside from Sullivan's dilemma, Murphy had another problem. Cliff Jones had forgotten his training gear. Before leaving their homes for London, the squad members were sent a letter by the Welsh FA telling them to bring their own training equipment for the tournament – boots, studs, shinguards, tops and gym shoes. Jones arrived empty-handed.

Jones had to return home to collect his gear. Fortunately, he had just moved to a London club, Tottenham, and lived, along with Tottenham team-mate Mel Hopkins, in Palmer's Green, north London. "I was always doing things like forgetting my kit," admits Jones. "I was a very forgetful person."

Following these two mishaps, a furious Murphy, read the riot act to the squad. He was used to the highest professional standards at Old Trafford where he and Busby ruled with an iron fist. Murphy accused the Welsh players of not taking the forthcoming World Cup seriously.

As Colin Webster, one of the self-confessed rogues in the squad, recalls, "To us the World Cup was just another cup competition. We didn't think it was that more special than the League or the FA Cup. Then, the World Cup wasn't like it is today. For a lot of us the best thing about it was that we were going to have a look at another country."

He recalls Murphy, sensing the players had become too laid back for their own good, cracking the whip in London. "He said just after we arrived 'Tomorrow is a free day' so I decided to have a lie-in. At 11am he kicked open the door to my hotel room and said 'Get up for training!' I said 'What happened to the free day?' He shouted back 'It's over!' Because I was a United player I used to get it in the neck more than the other players. If any of the players were missing, the first door he'd knock was mine."

For Murphy the problems did not end with Sullivan's forgotten passport and Jones's missing training gear. Tracksuits, maroon with Wales printed in white on the back, had been specially ordered. The players were supposed to wear them until the end of the World Cup but they had not arrived. Jack Jones, the Welsh trainer, had the unenviable task of asking staff at the FA's headquarters if he could borrow tracksuits until the new ones appeared.

Then it was off for training but even this had been reduced to a farce. Earlier that month, the Welsh FA had asked Finchley Football Club if the Welsh squad could train at their ground at Summers Lane. The ground had been recommended to the Welsh FA by

Stanley Rous, then secretary of the English FA. England had
planned to use Summers Lane but then decided on training at
Roehampton.

Finchley agreed to let the Welsh use their facilities, but on May 21,
eight days before the Welsh party's arrival in London, a letter arrived
at the Welsh FA's offices in Fairy Road, Wrexham. It was from
Finchley and the contents sent Herbert Powell into a spin. Apparently the groundsman at Finchley was unaware Wales planned to
train at Summers Lane and, since the football season had come to an
end, he had covered the pitch with top soil and grass seed. As a result,
Finchley was out of bounds.

Since the cancellation had come at such short notice, there was no
time to find an alternative venue. Murphy resorted to marching his
players, who were wearing a motley assortment of strips, across
Bayswater Road to Hyde Park – Wales's new pre-World Cup training ground.

While England manager Walter Winterbottom took his players to
the luxurious surrounds of the Bank of England Sports Club ground
in Roehampton, Wales had to settle for a public park in central London. It was a testament to Murphy's resolve that he did not flinch
from the prospect of parading his team past the commuters, tourists
and shoppers of the British capital. Ignoring the park's horseriders
and sunbathers, Murphy put his players through their paces. "We
put down two coats and used them as goalposts!" says Ken Jones.
"Our preparations were crap, absolutely rubbish. We looked like a
Mickey Mouse team. There was England training behind closed-
doors in one of the best places in the world, and there we were, carrying our gear under our arms and going to Hyde Park."

Medwin, too, was unimpressed with the set-up. "It wasn't the
best place to train, but we'd practised in far worse places abroad. At
least Hyde Park was flat, had grass and was close to the hotel. We
didn't abuse the place and our six-a-side and eight-a-side games
shouldn't have caused any problems. There weren't too many people there at the time and Jimmy took us to a secluded part of the
park."

There was one obstacle with Hyde Park. Ball games were banned.
Murphy spent the training session with his eyes peeled for park war-
dens. His luck ran out during a six-a-side practice match when a park
official tapped him on the shoulder. When Murphy told him they
were the Welsh World Cup squad and explained their plight, the
warden agreed to turn a blind eye.

While in London the players were measured-up for their World
Cup blazers at Simpson Ltd in Piccadilly. The Welsh FA had decided

on a black coloured blazer with the Welsh badge stitched on the left breast.

In Sweden, however, John Charles, would complain he was not as well-dressed as his team-mates. While they were being fitted in London the centre-forward was in Italy, still unsure whether the Italian FA would let him play in the World Cup. The selectors brought a blazer over for Charles but, because the Juventus star could not visit the store, the tailors had to gamble on his personal measurements. When Charles tried on his blazer, he had a nasty surprise.

"It was too small for me," laughs Charles. "The sleeves were half-way up my arms and it didn't cover my bottom. I felt really out of place." Ken Jones claims that soon after arriving in Soltsjöbaden an unhappy John Charles 'borrowed' some of his clothes. "He came with this small attaché case while I had a massive bag of clothes. He looked at my trousers and said, 'These will be all right'. I said to him, 'What am I going to wear? Take them off!' Do you know what John said? 'Well, take them off me then'. He was a huge bloke so I let it go. Luckily I had another pair of trousers, similar to the ones he'd taken."

Wales and England agreed to play a warm-up match behind closed doors at Roehampton before leaving British shores. The two countries were in danger of incurring the wrath of FIFA whose rules stated no teams taking part in the World Cup can play each other three weeks before the competition. With little more than a week before the opening matches, Murphy and Winterbottom were playing a dangerous game, but the English and Welsh officials agreed to stage it as a practice match and to play less than the full 90 minutes.

At Roehampton, Murphy experimented. Webster played centre-forward and Medwin outside-right but it was England who won the match thanks to a goal from West Bromwich Albion centre-forward Derek Kevan. Although England won, there was a marked difference between the two camps. The Welsh players, with no pressure on them at all, were relaxed and constantly joking. The English were tense and nervous. The burden placed on them by an expectant Fleet Street was starting to take its toll while Winterbottom, a good friend of Murphy's, was unsure of his best team.

One night, at the Lancaster Court, the pair were discussing the tournament. Winterbottom said he envied Murphy because the Welsh team picked itself since there were so few Welsh players of international class. "We have so many players to choose from that I've too many headaches," moaned Winterbottom. Murphy was not sympathetic. "Give me two of your headaches and I'll win the World Cup," he replied. Those two headaches were Bobby Charlton, a pupil of his at Manchester United, and Tom Finney. Charlton, incidentally, would not play a single game for England in Sweden.

On June 2, just after 1.30pm, BEA Flight 210 landed at Bromma Airport in Stockholm. "I nearly missed that flight," says Ken Jones. "At London I got onto the wrong plane. As the team were called to board the plane I went to get a newspaper. After I bought the paper I saw this crowd of people and I just followed them, thinking they were on our flight. When I got on the plane I didn't see anyone I recognised so I asked the stewardess 'Where's the Welsh team?' She said 'What team?' I said 'The Welsh team?' She didn't know what I was talking about. I said, 'This is the plane for Sweden, isn't it'. She said, 'Sweden? This is going to Tel Aviv'. I jumped off the plane and saw Jimmy Murphy further down the runway waving his fist at me. All the lads clapped when I came on board. It was only my third trip abroad."

At Bromma, the Welsh party – the players in their black blazers and the officials in their grey and brown suits – stepped onto the tarmac warmed by the day's brilliant sunshine. The Swedish welcoming party greeted them with a round of applause and a short speech while Milwyn Jenkins was presented with a bouquet of red, white and blue flowers. This, believing the Union Jack colours were also the Welsh colours, was the first of two errors the confused Swedes made regarding Wales's identity. Before each of Wales's World Cup games *God Save the Queen*, and not *Hen Wlad Fy Nhadau*, was played as the Welsh national anthem.

"We have had a very pleasant journey and all the boys are fit and well," said Herbert Powell on arrival in the Swedish capital. They passed through customs – the selectors allowed the players to bring 200 cigarettes each into Sweden, but no alcohol – before boarding the coach which would take them to their base, the Grand Hotel in Soltsjöbaden, a high-class resort 20 miles outside Stockholm. The players would train every morning at the Soltsjöbaden Athletic and Football Ground, around four miles from the hotel.

Just days after Wales had beaten Israel, Herbert Powell flew to Sweden to choose a suitable hotel for the team. He had made a good choice. The Grand Hotel, overlooking the Baltic Sea, was a millionaire's playground with a nine-hole golf course and tennis courts. It was considered one of the best hotels in the country. Before the World Cup, the Welsh FA had not excelled when it came to preparing for trips aboard. On this occasion, there could be no complaints. As Kelsey later recalled, "Someone told us there were 400 yachts on that lake. I never counted them myself but it could well have been true." But Ken Jones says, "They booked one of the best hotels only because they didn't think we were going to stay very long."

On arrival, the players were split into pairs to share a room. Colin Webster was twinned with Vic Crowe; Colin Baker with Ken Jones; Derrick Sullivan with Ken Leek; Trevor Edwards with Ron Hewitt; the Tottenham players, Mel Hopkins and Terry Medwin, were paired; captain David Bowen shared with Roy Vernon; Cliff Jones was put with Mel Charles, both Swansea men; Jack Kelsey shared with Stuart Williams and Ivor Allchurch shared with John Charles.

Soltsjöbaden was a favourite weekend destination for wealthy Swedes escaping the pressures of city life in Stockholm.

"It was a beautiful place and very relaxing," remembers Mel Charles. "It had a lovely little port and we would sit outside drinking lemonade. Jimmy wouldn't let us drink alcohol. He only allowed it at certain times, like after a match. We would train in the morning but in the afternoon we could do what we wanted. Some played golf, others took a trip into Stockholm."

Hewitt recalls, "It was the best hotel I've ever stayed in. While we were there we lived like kings, sunbathing and having a dip in the sea."

The hotel was just 20 yards from the Baltic and summer villas were dotted along the resort's coast. "We didn't want to leave the hotel," says Charles, who spent most of his time in Soltsjöbaden improving the already impressive tan he had caught in Italy. "When we had to go to Gothenburg to play Brazil in the quarter-final, we asked Jimmy if we could stay the night in the Grand and then fly to Gothenburg in the morning, but he said that wouldn't be possible."

Inevitably, there were difficulties in communication between the players and the obliging hotel staff. None of the Welsh players spoke Swedish while not all of the staff spoke English. The most bizarre incident involved a thirsty Ivor Allchurch who, after returning from a hard morning's training, telephoned room service and ordered two lemonades.

After 45 minutes nothing had arrived. Allchurch, presuming his order had been forgotten or misplaced, joined the rest of his colleagues for lunch. When he returned to room 21, he found two plates of bacon and eggs by his bed.

It was in Soltsjöbaden that 'the Big Five' was born, a clique within the squad made up of Sullivan, Webster, Baker, Leek and Ken Jones. Apart from Sullivan, these players had one thing in common – they were on the fringes of the first-team, although Sullivan, Jones and Baker were team-mates at Cardiff City and already good friends.

"We just seemed to hit it off," says Webster. "We weren't the elite.

That was Kelsey, Cliff, Ivor and John Charles. We classed ourselves
as outsiders. We went where the others didn't go." One of those
places, according to Webster, was the forest surrounding the Grand
Hotel. There 'the Big Five' would take a kit-bag full of beer. "We'd
have about three bottles each," says Webster. "We used to buy the
beer from this little off-licence 60 yards from the hotel and we'd carry
the bottles back in a kit-bag so Murphy wouldn't notice.

"If he had found out what we were up to he would have done his
nut. But we'd never get drunk. We just had enough to quench our
thirst." The empty beer bottles were hidden in the wardrobe in
Webster's room which he shared with Vic Crowe.

"I had to do that because nobody wanted to take them back to the
off-licence," says Webster. "After a while there were a good few bottles in that wardrobe, close to a hundred I'd say. I told the maid not
to open the wardrobe because if she did she'd get killed, but one day
she opened it and all the bottles fell out."

Ken Jones says, "At breakfast one of our five put a notice on a
table in the dining room – RESERVED FOR THE BIG FIVE
ONLY. I don't know who did it. We ate together, we drank together,
we trained together. We always drank in my room or Colin's. We
used to hire a boat and row to this island on the lake. We'd take a
packed lunch and stay there all day."

Webster points out that 'the Big Five' was not the only gang
within the squad. "There were other cliques. You had Ivor, Terry
and the other Swansea boys. You had John and Mel, the two brothers. There was Dave and Jack, who were both with Arsenal. We all
got on but we did different things in our free time. Some would stay
in the hotel, some would write letters. We always wanted to get out,
for a swim or for a walk around the lake.

"There were nude beaches near the hotel," recalls Webster.
"There was men only, mixed, and women only. One day Sulli and I
walked into the women's section. There were all these big, blonde
Swedish girls. I've never seen anything like it! I went sunbathing once
at 3am. Soltsjöbaden was close to the midnight sun. The early hours
of the morning over there meant it was like our dusk in Britain. It was
bloody freezing! I stayed for 20 minutes and then went back to the
hotel."

Ken Jones says some of the first-team players – the squad players
called them "the senior pros" – used 'the Big Five' to buy alcohol and
cigarettes. "Jack Kelsey would come up to me and say, 'Where are
you going this morning, Ken?' I'd tell him and then he'd say 'Do me a
favour. Get me a couple of bottles of beer'. I was the guinea pig. If the
selectors found out about me buying beer it would be me who would

take the rap, not Jack. The senior pros didn't want to risk getting caught, they didn't want their reputations tarnished. It wasn't just Jack who'd ask me. Mel Charles would, and Dave Bowen and John Charles and Stuart Williams. The senior pros would do their drinking in my room. They were too terrified of having beer in their own rooms."

The senior pros have their own memories of 'the Big Five'. Williams recalls, "I was walking along the lake one day with Jack Kelsey when we noticed these white things in the water bobbing up and down. We followed them along to this building and we could see these white things being thrown out of a window and into the water. We went inside and there were 'the Big Five' sitting down with bottles of beer and these white plastic cups from the hotel." John Charles adds, "I could hear these noises from my room all the time, coming from out the back – it was the noise of glass against glass. Then I'd hear a tap at a window. I'd look out and see the fella from the local shop outside Colin Webster's window, carrying a box of beer. They were even having it delivered to their hotel room."

Ken Jones recalls one night he made use of the window at the back of his room. "Ken Leek and I met these two Swedish girls by the lake one day. They were sisters and both very attractive. They invited us to their house to meet their parents. Their father was a doctor. A couple of days later, wearing our blazers, we went to see them. They lived high up in the mountains and Ken and I hired bicycles to get there. After a couple of hours we left because we had to get back to the hotel before lights out. We went bombing down the hill on these bikes but I forgot they were fixed-pedal so I couldn't stop the wheels. I lost control on a bend and hit this low wall. I went flying over it and landed in a cow pat.

"I couldn't go through the front door covered in muck so I sneaked round the back, tapped the window and asked Colin (Baker) to let me in. The next day I asked one of the hotel girls to wash the blazer in the laundry. I was without it for a few days and it was awkward because we had to wear blazers to all the matches. Luckily, I brought a white mac with me. They were all the rage at the time, and I wore that instead. A few people asked me where my blazer was. I said it was too short for me and that I was having a few alterations done on it."

Some of the players preferred the quiet life. "When I went somewhere I liked to look around because I'd never have the opportunity of going there again." says Hopkins. "I would walk around the woods or the lake, but I was in the minority. Most of the lads liked to play cards."

The players were given £28 spending money for the first two weeks, which worked out at £2 a-day. On his first night in Sweden, Ken Jones spent most of his World Cup allowance. As Ken Leek recalls, "We knew we'd be in Sweden for two weeks so Herbert Powell gave us all £28 spending money. On the first night Ken says, 'What shall we do?' We decided to go into Stockholm for a drink. After a while we decided to leave but Ken says, 'I'll stay here for a bit longer'. Anyway, at 3am there's a knock on my hotel door. It was Ken. He asked if he could borrow a fiver for the taxi because he'd spent his £28!" Jones explains what happened to his spending money. "I spent it all on this girl. She was a model. She had done some work for Colibri Lighters and I met her in a nightclub in Stockholm, but in the nightclubs over in Sweden you were expected to eat so I paid for dinner. Everything over there was so expensive. A cup of tea was 85p."

During the stay in the Swedish village, Murphy's regime was strict but relaxed.

"Jimmy made sure there were a few bottles of beer on the dinner table as well as orange juice, milk and water," remembers Medwin. "It was his way of saying you can have a drink without going mad. Because we appreciated that, the players hardly drank the beer and stuck to the other drinks." Hewitt adds, "Jimmy wasn't a nasty manager. He was hard, but he wasn't nasty. He managed to get the balance right." Murphy would spend around two hours training with his players every morning. He also held a one-hour talk with the squad to discuss the day's plans.

"Jimmy would say at the end, 'Anyone got any questions?' Nobody said a thing," says Hewitt. "That's how shy we all were."

At meal-times the players were fed either steak, chicken or fish. At night Murphy asked them to be in bed by 9.30pm to 10pm. "There was no real need for a curfew," says Webster, "because there wasn't much to do." Leek adds, "Training in the morning started at 9.30am or 10am, and finished at about midday. Jimmy was very thorough with the training. He'd have us doing six-a-sides, sprints, lapping, medicine ball work and the forwards would have shooting practice. After that you could do what you want. There was a club in the hotel, but Jimmy would only let us go in there after a game."

On their first night at the Grand Hotel, the players were joined by four unexpected guests, Milwyn Jenkins and five other Welsh FA officials. They had booked to stay at the Foresta Hotel, in Stockholm, in February, but within minutes of arriving there, the six stormed out. "We didn't get the rooms we wanted," said the Welsh FA chairman. "They were given to some Americans. I was put on the tenth floor. There was no lift so we walked out."

The players and the selectors were all under the same roof and relations were hardly harmonious.

"They never ate with us," says Mel Charles. "They had their own table away from where we sat and they stayed in another part of the hotel."

While the players slept in rooms two to 21 most of the selectors stayed in rooms 128–131.

"You couldn't talk to them about football, they knew nothing about the game. One of the selectors was a roadsweeper, another was a toilet attendant. I'll tell you how little they knew about the game," says Charles. "One of the selectors came to see me once, when I was playing for Arsenal. We were at Everton and I was supposed to be playing centre-forward, but I was injured. Jeff String wore the number nine shirt instead of me and he scored a goal that day. A few weeks later I was playing for Wales against Scotland at Ninian Park and the selector came up to me and said, 'What a wonderful goal you scored against Everton, Mel.' He couldn't even recognise me! I didn't have the heart to say it wasn't me playing."

Ken Jones had also experienced the selectors' lack of knowledge during the five-day stay in London. "Mel (Charles) and I arrived at the Kensington Park Hotel in a taxi from Paddington. We entered the hotel and there were the selectors drinking coffee. They greeted Mel. Then they saw me, turned to Mel and asked, 'Mel, who is this with you?' He told them 'Ken Jones'. They said, 'Ken Jones?' And Mel replied, 'Ken Jones, the goalkeeper'. It was like something out of *Dad's Army* or Charles Dickens. Unbelievable. And the Welsh nation was relying on that lot to pick the team. They would only talk to John Charles, or Jack Kelsey or Dave Bowen. They wouldn't talk to the lesser players."

Webster, too, has nothing good to say about the selectors running Welsh football at the time. "When they walked into the hotel games room we'd just walk out. We kept out of their way. They didn't even know which player was which. They would go up to Ivor Allchurch and say 'Who are you?' The only player they recognised was John (Charles) and that's only because he was so big. Powell, the secretary, would bring his sister on all the trips and one of the selectors, a chap called George Owens (he was also the Welsh FA treasurer), wore trousers which had creases on the sides. I remember him asking one of the players which town Tottenham was in." Out of all the selectors it is Owens that the 1958 survivors remember best. "He looked like a tramp," says Ken Jones. "What an advert for Wales he was. His jacket looked like he'd been sleeping in it." Hopkins adds, "He was a little bald guy from North Wales. He kept sticking his tongue out. He was like a comic. The only selector who knew anything about the game was Fred Dewey. You could talk about football with Dewey. The others didn't even know who you were. They were just shop-keepers. They kept getting me and Mel Charles mixed up. They called me Mel Charles and Mel Charles they called Mel Hopkins.

"Powell was an old-fashioned bachelor. He ruled the roost. The selectors did what he said. He was the scoutmaster, they were the cubs. Jimmy Murphy used to keep as far away from the selectors as possible. He was one of the lads. He liked mixing with the players."

Webster remembers the selectors' behaviour during the 100 mile coach trip from Soltsjöbaden to Sandviken, where Wales played their first World Cup match against Hungary.

"They were a Bible-preaching bunch. They told us that during the journey there was to be no smoking on the bus and that we all had to sing Welsh hymns! There was no way we were singing hymns. If we sang it was usually songs by Charles McDevitt and Nancy Whiskey but there we were, on the way to play Hungary and the selectors and their wives were singing hymns.

"The no smoking thing really got to Jack (Kelsey), but he'd still light up. He would inhale from the cigarette and then puff out of the window to avoid being caught. Jack would smoke 10 cigarettes dur-ing a match if he had the chance.

"I smoked on the trip. I didn't smoke much but I always had a couple before a match. It helped relax me. The crazy thing was that there seemed to be more selectors than players. There were 18 players and 16 officials! It was crazy."

To maintain match fitness and boost morale, Wales arranged two warm-up matches with the local side, Soltsjöbaden, who played in the third division of the Stockholm and District League. Practice matches against local club sides had become popular in the 1958 World Cup. France played three sides from the Kopparberg area and won all three 12–0, 14–0 and 13–1. Yugoslavia hammered a village side 11–0 and Sweden, too, joined the party beating one team 8–0.

Kelsey suggested to Murphy that in both games with Soltsjöbaden, the amateur opponents ought to be given a goal start, as a sign of sportsmanship. Murphy, ever competitive, refused. The first match was played on the Wednesday night, four days before the clash with Hungary. It was supposed to be behind closed-doors but several Swedish journalists, eager to catch a glimpse of the competi-tion's rank outsiders and their country's final opponents in Group Three, had sneaked into the tiny ground.

Among the handful of observers was Dr Sten Lilgedahl, who had been sent by Sweden's manager George Raynor to spy on Wales. The mind games had well and truly begun and Murphy was not to be out-done. Accompanied by his captain, Bowen, he would board a motor-boat at Soltsjöbaden and head for the Swedish camp at nearby Lillsved, on the Baltic passage, to study the Swedish players during training.

Wales, not surprisingly, walloped poor Soltsjöbaden 15–0. Colin Webster scored four, Hewitt and Jones both three, Leek and Medwin two each and Allchurch one. The second-half was played in heavy rain. The second match, two days later, was played in public. Wales did even better, winning 19–0. This time Allchurch scored seven, Jones six, John Charles four and Medwin two.

The idea of arranging warm-up massacres against amateur oppo-sition nearly backfired on the Welsh. In the second game John Charles fell heavily going for goal. Murphy's heart was in his mouth. Charles appeared hurt but carried on. He had suffered a swollen knee but would recover in time for the Hungary match 48 hours later.

Many questioned the merits of these two matches. It was doubtful whether Soltsjöbaden could offer any resistance to a Sunday morn-ing park side, let alone a national team that had qualified, albeit through the back door, for the World Cup.

But Kelsey, a mere bystander in both warm-ups, defended the decision, "The two games served a good purpose, if only as a confi-dence builder," he said. Kelsey recalled the effect an easy warm-up match had on the Hungarians before their famous friendly against England in November 1953. En route to London they stopped in Paris to play the Renault car factory team. Puskas and company won 13–0 and the memory of their dire performance against Sweden, in Budapest a few days earlier, was wiped out. Hungary then went on to beat England 6–3 at Wembley.

Murphy was hoping the same would happen for Wales. Except for the two Israel matches, results so far in 1958 had not been good. Maybe a couple of landslide victories, albeit against third-rate oppo-sition, would provide a much-needed fillip for the players.

As it happened they scored 34 goals without reply. The mood on the bus trip to Sandviken, where Hungary awaited, was one of quiet confidence.

CHAPTER SIX

THE CONTENDERS

IN Sweden, 16 teams would do battle for the Jules Rimet Trophy, a far cry from the first ever tournament, in Uruguay in 1930, when 13 countries took part. Only four sides from Europe – France, Yugoslavia, Romania and Belgium – bothered to make that mammoth journey to South America. The prospect of a month at sea crossing the Atlantic did not appeal.

Britain, too, treated Frenchman Jules Rimet's brainchild with contempt. It was not until the 1950 World Cup in Brazil that a British side appeared in the competition. That was England who, for their trouble, were humiliated by the USA in a famous match in Belo Horizonte, a match England lost 1–0.

The 1958 World Cup, however, was the first true World Cup. There were 16 teams in 1950 and again in Switzerland in 1954, but for the sixth finals in Sweden every major football power had tried to qualify. This was what Rimet had dreamed of in 1930. Sadly, he was not alive to see his dream fulfilled. The former FIFA president died in October 1956.

The Soviet Union, making their first ever World Cup appearance, were one of three sides from behind the Iron Curtain. The others were Czechoslovakia and Hungary. Argentina were appearing in the tournament for the first time since 1934. Also from Latin America were Brazil, Paraguay and Mexico. Austria had qualified, so too France and Yugoslavia. Then there were the two nations that qualified without having to kick a ball, West Germany as holders and Sweden as hosts. For the first time all four British teams had qualified – England, Scotland, Wales and Northern Ireland. It has never happened since.

The draw had been made in Zürich on February 9. This time FIFA dispensed with seeding the strongest teams together and opted for geographical seeding. This was made convenient since the 16 nations were made up of four from Britain, four from Western

Europe, four from Eastern Europe and four from South/Central America. The four groups would have one team from each.

Northern Ireland were drawn with West Germany, Czechoslovakia and Argentina in Group One; Scotland faced France, Yugoslavia and Paraguay in Group Two; Wales were drawn with Sweden, Hungary and Mexico in Group Three; England had Brazil, the Soviet Union and Austria in Group Four.

Wales were considered one of the no-hopers. They were a team lucky to qualify, a team in Sweden to make up the numbers. As Jack Kelsey wryly commented after the World Cup, nobody expected Wales to score a single goal, let alone win a match. After a week, when the first-round games had finished, the Welsh would almost certainly be on the first flight back to London.

"None of us thought we'd get past the first-round," admits Webster. "It was just an adventure for us. Don't get me wrong, we worked hard, but for most of us Sweden was just a nice trip." Two teams qualified from each group, the winner and the runners-up. If teams tied for the runners-up spot then the outcome would be decided by a play-off match, not goal difference.

"To be honest, I thought we'd be going home after a week," adds Mel Charles. "We had some very good players but deep down I thought Sweden and Hungary would go through." Hewitt agrees. "I didn't think we'd get done," he says, "but I didn't think we'd reach the quarter-finals." Hopkins was another of the pessimists. "It was going to be a hard tournament and we were in a tough group. Only two of the British sides were given a chance and they were England and Scotland."

Wales's record on foreign soil was hardly earth-shattering. In 25 years, Wales had played 10 games abroad and three of those were in Paris. The record was nine defeats and one draw. That miserable run came to an end in the play-off match in Tel Aviv when Israel were beaten 2–0. The Welsh had tried to qualify for the 1950 and 1954 tournaments. Then, the four British sides played each other to determine who travelled to Brazil and Switzerland but Wales and Northern Ireland lost out to England and Scotland on both occasions.

"We were badly organised for a competition like the World Cup where good preparation is half the battle," says Cliff Jones. "Jimmy hadn't been able to study any of our opponents, we'd had very little practice together and when we flew out we weren't even sure John Charles would play for us."

Terry Medwin, however, says he was optimistic Wales could reach the quarter-finals.

"With two teams progressing out of four you've got to feel you've got a chance. Sweden may have been the hosts but they were not the best European side and Mexico were hardly Brazil or Argentina. We had a lot of experienced players and they all played for good clubs."

It was easy to see why the Swedes and Hungarians were expected to make the last eight. Sweden would be roared on by a partisan crowd in the Swedish capital, Stockholm. They also boasted a clutch of world-class players who plied their trade in Italy's Serie A. George Raynor, their Yorkshire-born manager, confidently predicted they would reach the final. Hungary were runners-up in the last World Cup, in Switzerland, and even though they had lost most of their best players after the Hungarian Uprising in 1956, they were still considered a force. One of their warm-up games was against Scotland at Glasgow. The Hungarians earned a 1–1 draw, a good result considering Scotland had also qualified for Sweden.

Murphy admitted that because of commitments at Old Trafford he was unable to spy on Wales's opponents. Nevertheless, he feared no nasty surprises. The 4–2–4 formation had become the rage in 1958 and this had been practised by Herbert Chapman's Arsenal two decades earlier. Murphy was more than familiar with this strategy.

All four British sides had been affected by the Munich air disaster. Wales lost Murphy's undivided attention as well as 18–year-old winger and wonderkid Ken Morgans, but without doubt England were the worst hit by the tragedy. Walter Winterbottom, England's manager since 1946, lost three key players – left-back Roger Byrne, left-half Duncan Edwards and centre-forward Tommy Taylor. In effect, Winterbottom lost the backbone of the team.

Byrne was reputedly the fastest left-back in the world. Only John Charles was considered a better player in the air than Taylor. The powerful Edwards, who made his international debut at 17, was the finest footballer of his generation. At United, Murphy described Edwards as the "Kohinoor diamond amongst our crown jewels". Three months before he died, Edwards had finished third in the European Footballer of the Year poll, behind Real Madrid's Alfredo di Stefano and Billy Wright of Wolves.

Their replacements, Tommy Banks of Bolton Wanderers, Billy Slater of Wolves and Derek Kevan of West Bromwich Albion, although good club players, were pale shadows of the United trio.

Murphy always maintained that had Byrne, Taylor and Edwards played in the 1958 tournament, England, and not Brazil, would have won the trophy. The repercussions of Munich did not end there for Winterbottom. The crash had badly affected Bobby Charlton, the young midfielder of whom so much was expected. He returned to play for United a month after the disaster and was included in the

England squad that flew to Sweden. But Charlton was mentally and physically exhausted after a tortuous four months and he would not play in any of England's matches.

England, who flew over 20 players, were one of four teams that did not bring their full quota of playing staff to Sweden – Wales, with 18, Czechoslovakia with 16 and Northern Ireland with 15, were the other three. England were also the last team to arrive in Sweden, just three days before their opening match against the Soviet Union.

Three players surprisingly omitted from the squad were winger Stanley Matthews and two centre-forwards, Nat Lofthouse and Brian Clough. Matthews, despite being 43, was playing as well as ever for Blackpool while Lofthouse, nicknamed 'the Lion of Vienna' after his match-winning display in Austria six years earlier, had scored both Bolton's goals in the 1958 FA Cup final. Clough had many supporters following a terrific season with Middlesbrough in the Second Division.

England qualified unbeaten from a relatively easy qualifying group, one which involved the Republic of Ireland and Denmark, to reach the finals. Despite the tragic loss of Byrne, Edwards and Taylor, and the absence of Matthews and Lofthouse, they were still considered one of the favourites to lift the World Cup. At right-back was Don Howe of West Bromwich Albion, at centre-half, and playing in his third World Cup, was Billy Wright. On the wings were Bryan Douglas of Blackburn Rovers and Tom Finney of Preston and in attack were the two Fulham forwards, Bobby Robson and Johnny Haynes. It was an impressive line-up.

The English base was the modern Park Avenue Hotel in Gothenburg – the seaport city known as 'Little London' – where they would play two of their three first-round matches. If Winterbottom looked a worried man he could be forgiven. Just before the World Cup draw in February, he said the two teams he feared most were the Soviet Union and Brazil. England were drawn to face both nations in Group Four. Also occupying his mind was England's 5–0 defeat against fellow finalists Yugoslavia the previous month, in a friendly in Belgrade. It gave their first-round opponents a huge lift and proved the English were far from invincible.

Besides England, the other fancied British side were Scotland who arrived in Sweden keen to lay the ghost of 1954. Then, the Scots were involved in their first World Cup. It proved to be a nightmare as they lost both first-round games, 1–0 to Austria and, humiliatingly, 7–0 to Uruguay. The Scots, in fact, had qualified for the 1950 competition but, because they finished second to England in their qualifying group, decided not to take part.

Scotland, too, had been hit by the Munich tragedy. Unlike England they did not lose any players. They lost a manager – Matt Busby. In November 1957, after Scotland's 3–2 victory over Switzerland at Hampden Park, a victory that sealed Scotland's place in the finals, the Scottish FA approached Busby about leading his country in Sweden. Busby accepted. Three months later, he was critically injured in the Munich crash. He made a remarkable recovery but was in no fit state to manage a side competing in the World Cup.

It was a huge blow for the Scots. Busby had made United the best team in the land and his tactical know-how and presence would have made a huge difference. Scotland arrived for their second World Cup without a manager. All team matters were, ominously, in the hands off the much-criticised selectors who, prior to the World Cup, had been accused of not producing a settled Scottish side. On only three occasions in the last four years had the selectors fielded the same side twice. The players were also low on morale. Although Scotland had done well to pip Spain in their qualifying group, they were brought down to earth with a friendly against 'the Auld Enemy' in April.

On home soil, at Hampden Park in Glasgow, England walloped the Scots 4–0 in one of the most one-sided encounters between the two nations. For Scotland, it was a disastrous dress-rehearsal for Sweden although a 2–1 friendly win in Poland the following month restored some confidence.

The 1958 squad included some talented players such as full-backs Tommy Docherty of Preston and John Hewie of Charlton, centre-half Bobby Evans of Celtic and inside-right Jimmy Murray of Hearts, although the great Scottish hope was Celtic's brilliant inside-forward, Bobby Collins.

The Scottish party were based in the same hotel as the Welsh, in the Grand Hotel in Soltsjöbaden. It was a curious choice since Scotland were playing their first-round games in Västeras, Norrköping and Örebro, all a long bus ride from Soltsjöbaden.

Northern Ireland's route to the finals was as remarkable and dramatic as Wales's. In a qualifying group which included twice-winners Italy and Portugal they had been given no chance of reaching Sweden.

However, in May 1957, Northern Ireland threw their hat in the ring by thumping Portugal 3–0 at Belfast's Windsor Park. The home match with Italy in December would decide everything. That match was supposed to have been refereed by the Hungarian Istvan Zsolt but bad weather at London Airport meant Zsolt and his two linesmen could not fly to Belfast for the vital qualifier. The stand-by officials were called in. The only problem was that the stand-by referee, Tommy Mitchell, was an Irishman.

The Italians protested claiming the referee must be neutral. The Northern Irish FA agreed but rather than postpone the match it was played as a friendly – or a not-so-friendly as it turned out. A bad-tempered 90 minutes, which saw Italy's Giuseppe Chiappella sent off, ended 2–2.

The all-important qualifier was replayed in January 1958 and Northern Ireland triumphed 2–1. They had qualified for the World Cup. Italy, winners in 1934 and 1938, were staying home.

Astonishingly, Northern Ireland very nearly withdrew from the tournament because of a little-known clause in their FA's own rulebook. It said the national team was banned from playing on a Sunday – and in Sweden two of their first-round games, the opener against the Czechs and the last against West Germany, were Sunday matches.

The selectors alerted FIFA to their plight but FIFA refused to alter the World Cup schedule. Northern Ireland ignored the "thou shall not play on the Sabbath" rule, but some of the FA officials, clearly unhappy about the situation, remained home in protest.

As with Wales, little was expected of Northern Ireland who were managed by the charismatic Doncaster Rovers manager Peter Doherty. Out of the four British teams, these two were the least likely to progress.

The Munich disaster had affected Northern Ireland, robbing them of centre-half Jackie Blanchflower who had not recovered from the crash. Murphy was one of many managers who rated Jackie, as talented as his more famous brother, Danny, the latter would captain the Northern Ireland side in Sweden. Doherty, though, was still able to call on United's brilliant goalkeeper Harry Gregg.

Doherty had built his team around Gregg and the outstanding Tottenham right-half and 1958 Footballer of the Year Danny Blanchflower (who famously described his team's strategy in Sweden as "to equalise before the other team scores") but these were by no means Northern Ireland's only quality players.

There was Wilbur Cush, the Leeds man who could play wing-half, centre-half and inside-forward, Celtic's left-half Bert Peacock, Burnley's talented inside-forward, Jimmy McIlroy, and Aston Villa's leggy winger, Peter McParland. Little wonder Sweden's shrewd and wily manager, Raynor, had tipped Northern Ireland to do well in the World Cup.

Doherty, like Murphy, was a renowned motivator of players and like his Welsh counterpart he made the best of limited resources. The

Irish were based in the Tylösands Havsbad, in Tylösand, on the west coast of Sweden. The selectors had chosen well. The hotel was reputed to be the best seaside hotel in the country, boasting stunning tennis courts as well as Sweden's finest golf course.

The holders, West Germany, had chosen the quiet village of Bjärred, near Malmö, as their headquarters. Four years earlier, in Switzerland, they had surprisingly beaten Puskas's Hungary 3–2 to win the World Cup for the first time in their history. The Germans, managed by the fierce-looking Sepp Herberger who had led them to glory in Berne, could not be discounted even though this was a much-changed side to the one which triumphed in Switzerland.

Only four of the 1954 side were still around – wingers Hans Schäfer and Helmut Rahn, right-half Horst Eckel and inside-forward and captain Fritz Walter. Walter was 37. Herberger had three exciting young players to unleash on the world stage, utility defender Karl-Heinz Schnellinger, left-half Horst Szymaniak and the stocky centre-forward from Hamburg, Uwe Seeler.

The Soviet Union were also among the favourites, despite never appearing in the World Cup before. The Russians had always refused to take part in international competitions until Stalin's death in 1953. Managed by Gabriel Katchaline, the Russians were feared. They had won the Olympic title in Melbourne in 1956 and they were impressive against England in a World Cup warm-up in Moscow. Also, Dynamo Moscow impressed during a British tour in 1945. Against Chelsea at Stamford Bridge, where the spectators laughed at the Russians for handing their English opponents bouquets of flowers before the kick-off, they drew 3–3. Then they massacred Cardiff City 10–1, beat Arsenal 4–3 and rounded off a sensational visit by drawing 2–2 with Rangers.

The Soviets chose Hindas, near Gothenberg, as their base. In the side was the formidable goalkeeper Lev Yashin, who played in black. But the Soviets, despite being many people's tip, had their problems. Igor Netto, the left-half and Soviet captain, was unfit to play in the early matches while Katchaline had lost three promising players who were appearing in court in Moscow for misbehaving at parties in the Soviet capital.

Much was expected of another Iron Curtain nation, Czechoslovakia, who had replaced Hungary as the outstanding team from Eastern Europe. The powerful Czechs, staying in the fashionable seaside resort of Bastad, were made up mostly of Dukla Prague players, the most influential of whom was left-back and captain Ladislav Novák. Left-half Josef Masopust and inside-right Milan Dvorak were ones to watch, while in defence they boasted the giant centre-half Jan Popluhár and right-back Jan Hertl.

They had qualified impressively, ahead of Wales and East Germany, and were considered one of Europe's up-and-coming teams, but it was unlikely they would qualify from a group which included West Germany and Argentina.

France, staying in the steel town of Finspang and managed by Paul Nicolas, were another of Europe's more interesting contenders although few believed they were capable of winning the greatest prize in football since they had failed to win a match in 1958. They arrived in Scandinavia nearly three weeks before the opening match, well before any of the other nations. They would be no pushovers. The bulk of the squad played for Rheims, the French side that reached the European Cup final two years earlier. The French qualified without losing a match but how well they would do depended on the two forwards, Raymond Kopa and Just Fontaine. Kopa was expected to be one of the competition's stars. He played for the all-conquering Real Madrid side while Moroccan-born Fontaine was a virtual unknown but how that would change over the next three weeks. He would go on to score 13 goals in the 1958 tournament, a record that will surely never be beaten. He was supposed to travel to Sweden as a reserve but when first-choice René Bliard was injured during training Fontaine took his place.

Sweden, on home soil and with a clutch of players which had set Italian football alight, had a great chance of winning the trophy for the first time, less so Hungary whose best players – Puskas, Kocsis et al – fled their mother country following the Hungarian Uprising in 1956.

The dark horses were perhaps the Yugoslavs who were based in the industrial city of Västeras, east of Stockholm. They boasted a decent record in the World Cup. Semi-finalists in 1930, they had also done well in 1950 and 1954. In the latter tournament they held Brazil 1–1 in a first-round match. Yugoslav football was renowned for its skill and the 1958 side boasted four exciting players, wing-half Vujadin Boskov, inside-left Dragoslav Sekularac and forwards Milos Milutinovic and Todor Veselinovic.

Little was expected of the remaining European side, Austria, which was perhaps unfair since, like England and France, the Austrians were undefeated in their qualifying group. Surprisingly, the selectors had not called up the experienced centre-half Ernst Ocwirk, who was playing in Italy with Sampdoria and who had played so well in the 1954 competition when Austria reached the last four. Ocwirk aside, the bulk of the 1954 side was still around in Sweden but in a tough group, arguably the toughest of the four, the Austrians were expected to be the fall guys.

From the other side of the world came Brazil, Argentina, Paraguay and Mexico.

Brazil, managed by the plump Vicente Feola and based at Hindas, within walking distance of the Russian camp, were installed as undisputed favourites. The squad, which included Gilmar, Nilton Santos, Didi, Vavà, Garrincha, Zagallo and a promising 17–year-old called Pelé, was one to fear.

But were they overrated? Brazil, after all, had not qualified that easily. They only had to face Peru after Venezuela withdrew. Against the Peruvians they drew 1–1 in Lima and then won the all-important return leg in Rio de Janeiro 1–0 thanks to a Didi free-kick.

The decade had been unkind to the men in canary yellow. In 1950, in the newly-built Maracana in Rio, a nation was reduced to tears when Uruguay beat the hosts 2–1 in the final. In 1954 Brazil were knocked-out by the Hungarians in the infamous Battle of Berne, one of the most violent matches in the competition's history. Brazil, in 1958, had much to prove.

Then there was Argentina, appearing in the competition for the first time since Italy in 1934. They, like Brazil, had high hopes in Sweden.

Their absence from the world scene was down to the Peron government which had ruled Argentina since 1946. It recommended the team did not compete in the 1950 and 1954 World Cups for fear of defeat. Defeat on the pitch would, Peron thought, turn the nation against his administration. However, in 1955 President Juan Peron was overthrown by the military, and the ban on competing in international competitions was lifted.

In Sweden, the Argentinians were managed by Guillermo Stàbile, one of his country's stars in the 1930 tournament when they lost 4–2 to Uruguay in the final in Montevideo. Stàbile finished as top scorer with eight goals and became the first man to score a World Cup hat-trick when Argentina thrashed Mexico 6–3.

Argentina, based in Ramlösa Hälsobrunn, just outside Hälsingborg, were expected to be a force in Sweden. In a qualifying group which included Chile and Bolivia they came through with ease, scoring 11 goals in the process. They were also reigning South American champions after winning the Copa America in Peru in 1957. It was the manner of the victory that made the world sit up and take notice. Brazil were thumped 3–0, Uruguay 4–0, Colombia 8–2 and Chile 6–2.

After the stunning Copa America success, the wealthy Italian clubs flew to Argentina and signed the country's three best players, Omar Sivori, Humberto Maschio and Antonio Angelillo (they were famously known as 'the Angels with Dirty Faces'). Sivori joined Juventus, Maschio joined Bologna and Angelillo moved to Inter. These three players, instrumental in the triumph in Peru, no longer played for Argentina which meant a much weakened side would kick-off the first match against West Germany.

Paraguay and Mexico were not considered threats although Paraguay, having qualified ahead of twice-winners Uruguay, deserved respect. In Florencio Amarilla, Jose Parodi and Jorgelino Romero they had some gifted forwards and they proved their worth in a 5–0 home win over the fading Uruguayans. Paraguay had chosen Sundbyholms Slott, a castle on Lake Mälaren, near Västeras, as their headquarters. Mexico were staying in Bosön, near Stockholm. They were considered the most mysterious team in the series – and by far the weakest contender from Latin America.

Out of the 16 teams, Argentina, West Germany, France, Yugoslavia, Sweden, Hungary, Brazil and England were expected to reach the last eight.

Northern Ireland, Czechoslovakia, Paraguay, Scotland, Mexico, Wales, the Soviet Union and Austria were favourites for the first flight home.

If there was to be an upset it would come from Czechoslovakia or the Soviet Union, maybe Paraguay. As for Wales, nobody gave them a prayer.

CHAPTER SEVEN

MAD MAGYARS

ON June 5, three days before the crunch opening match with Hungary, the telephone in Jimmy Murphy's hotel room rang. It was in the early hours of the morning and the noise woke the Welsh manager. He picked up the receiver. On the other end of the line was a member of the Swedish FA organising the matchday programme for the Wales-Hungary game on Sunday evening.

"Please," said the voice on the other end of the line, "we must haff your team. The programme must be printed wizout delay." Murphy could scarcely believe his ears. There was no way he was going to reveal his hand to his opposite number, Lajos Baroti. He wanted to keep his formation secret until the last minute.

"No other manager has named his team yet. You go to blazes!" shouted Murphy, before slamming down his phone. A few hours later a worried Gert Landine, the Welsh party's bespectacled nationsattaché (official team liaison officer) approached Murphy and pleaded with him to name his team for Sunday. "They are insisting. They are getting the Hungarian line-up for the programme too."

Murphy stood his ground. "You'll get no team out of me tonight. I don't even know it myself yet. If they must have a team then you pick it." And that is exactly what happened. Landin picked the Wales XI for the programme, which explained the eccentric line-up. Derrick Sullivan, a wing-half, was put in at outside-right. Terry Medwin, an outside-right, was named at left-back. Ron Hewitt, an inside-right who would not even play against Hungary, was right-back. Stuart Williams, a right-back, was named at left-half and Mel Hopkins, a left-back, was down as the outside-right. Only six of the players were named in their normal positions. If Wales did eventually surprise the 1954 runners-up then the unwitting Landin would deserve much of the credit.

Hungary and Wales would meet in Sandviken, a modern, industrial town in northern Sweden. Just 330 miles from the Arctic Circle, it has the honour of being the most northern venue ever used for a World Cup match. The 20,000 capacity stadium, the Jernvallen (the Iron Ground), was, with its bland main stand, untidy dirt track and grass mounds for spectators to stand on, the most basic and unimpressive of the 13 stadiums used in the 1958 World Cup.

The Hungarian team which would grace the Jernvallen was not the same as the one which took the 1954 tournament by storm. Then, with a team which included Puskas, Kocsis, Czibor, Hidegkuti, Budai and Bozsik, the Mighty Magyars swept all before them and reached the final which they surprisingly lost to West Germany despite racing into a 2–0 lead.

But in Sweden a number of sides had been weakened by losing a block of important players. England, through the Munich air crash, was one. Argentina, who had become a poaching ground for Italian clubs, was another. But the worst affected contender was Hungary.

In October 1956, the people of Hungary, led by former Prime Minister Imre Nagy, turned against the country's Soviet-supported dictatorship. It became known as the Hungarian Uprising. Riots broke out in every town and city and the revolt was ruthlessly tamed by Soviet tanks and troops. At the time Honved, Hungary's crack army team, which included the bulk of the Mighty Magyars such as Puskas, Kocsis, Czibor and Budai, was touring abroad. Following the violent and bloody events back home the core of this extraordinary team decided to exile themselves. The majority decided on Spain. Puskas joined Real Madrid while Kocsis and Czibor both joined Barcelona. Never again would they play for Hungary.

Not all the players stayed away. The 1958 side contained three survivors from 1954. Gyula Grosics, the goalkeeper, Jozsef Bozsik, the attacking wing-half and Nandor Hidegkuti, the deep-lying centre-forward who hit a hat-trick in the 6–3 defeat of England at Wembley five years earlier. Grosics thought hard about staying in the west but decided on a return home while it was no surprise to see Bozsik, a member of the Hungarian House of Representatives, refuse to join Puskas and the rest of the rebels. Hidegkuti was part of the MTK Budapest team which, like Honved, was abroad playing prestige matches when the uprising began. He returned to Hungary because his family lived there.

Even though these players were in Sweden they were past their peak. Grosics and Bozsik were 32 and Hidegkuti a ripe old 36. Hidegkuti, in fact, was at the centre of a row in the Hungarian camp on the eve of the Wales match. The row involved Hungary's manager Lajos Baroti, who had replaced Gustav Sebes, the man who guided the Magyars to the 1954 final, and the president of the Hungarian

FA, Sandor Barcs. Baroti claimed the centre-forward had eaten too much during the squad's two-week stay in Finland where they had prepared for the tournament. Hidegkuti had, apparently, developed a penchant for fried fish in Finland and was now four pounds overweight. Since they had arrived in Sweden the MTK player was put on a crash diet, but had lost just one pound. Baroti believed he was in no condition to play against the Welsh. Barcs, however, thought differently. What Hidegkuti lost in pace he would make up in craft, he said. After all, he had been part of the Golden Squad of the early Fifties.

There was no such strife in the Welsh camp. The mood was one of confidence, especially now the Italian FA had given John Charles permission to play in the tournament. Baroti had his fingers crossed that Charles would not be playing. When he discovered Charles would be there, Hungary's manager fell into an instant depression. "This will make our task much more difficult," he said. "Our clash with Wales will be a key game. If we are successful in this important match, I'm sure we'll make the quarter-finals. Otherwise, we'll probably be eliminated in the first-round." Baroti felt Hungary's defence was stronger than in 1954, but the attack weaker.

The Hungarians were favourites to beat Wales and qualify along with Sweden. Nevertheless, they were a side there for the taking. Before leaving Budapest airport for Finland a few weeks earlier, the players, hoping to buy goods not freely available in their home country, allegedly had money confiscated by Hungarian police. This hardly improved morale among the squad, while their last warm-up performance, a 5–1 win over Finland, was anything but impressive. Now there was the row between Baroti and Barcs.

Jozsef Bencsics, one of Hungary's midfield players, did his best to paper over the cracks. "The team is better than people in Sweden think it is," he said, "and we are confident of making good progress." Hungary did have new talent – left-winger Mate Fenyvesi, the tall centre-forward Lajos Tichy and his tricky partner in attack, Karoly Sándor. Whether they were in the same class as their 1954 predecessors – the likes of Puskas and Kocsis – remained to be seen.

For this match everything appeared to be going against Wales. First, they lost the right to wear their home colours. A couple of days earlier, FIFA officials had tossed a coin to decide which team would wear its change strip since both countries' colours were red shirts and white shorts. Hungary won, Wales would have to wear all yellow. "We are disappointed," captain Bowen said after the toss, "but it won't make any difference to our fighting spirit."

Then there was the coach journey. The Welsh, based in
Soltsjöbaden, had a three-hour trip to reach Sandviken. The
Hungarians, however, were based in the town, at the modern
Stadshotellet. While the Welsh squad played cards or slept on the
bus, the Hungarians were warming-up in the Jernvallen. After all,
their hotel was less than two miles from the ground.

"I remember that journey," says John Charles. "It seemed to last
forever. It went on and on and on. It was hardly the best preparation
before a World Cup match. We stepped off the coach and there were
the Hungarians training. With us it was a case of getting off the bus
and then getting changed for the match." Kelsey, in fact, recalled the
Hungarians having a full half-hour warm-up session before the
kick-off. "It was a bloody awful trip," says Hopkins. "It was a hot
day and in 1958 the transport was not good. There was no
air-conditioning, no TV or toilets on the coach. The trip was a real
slog. By the time we got there I thought we were going to get absolutely hammered."

Cliff Jones remembers stepping off the coach and seeing the
Hungarians limbering up. "I was looking at some of their players and
they did look useful." Jones searched for his marker, the lanky
full-back, Sandor Mátrai. "He could sprint," recalls Jones. "He was
going like the wind. I thought I was going to have my work cut out
that day."

Murphy defended Wales's decision to choose a hotel near Stockholm rather than joining the Hungarians in Sandviken. "You can't
fault us for staying in Soltsjöbaden because our next two games are
in the capital," he explained.

For this match Murphy toyed with the idea of playing the two
Charles brothers in attack with Derrick Sullivan replacing Mel at
centre-half and Vic Crowe filling in for Sullivan at right-half. The
Charles brothers had played together as forwards once before,
against England at Wembley in November 1956. It looked a useful
pairing. John Charles had given Wales the lead, but an injury to Mel
meant Murphy had to shuffle his pack and Wales eventually lost 3–1.

Murphy decided to keep Mel at centre-half. It would need a big,
powerful defender to nullify Tichy. The team Murphy named for
Wales's first ever World Cup match read: Kelsey, Williams,
Hopkins, Sullivan, Mel Charles, Bowen, Webster, Medwin, John
Charles, Allchurch, Jones. There were no real surprises except that
Medwin, a winger, was put at inside-right, and Webster, a forward,
was at outside-right.

"We all knew Hungary had lost players because of the uprising,"
says Medwin. "But they still had some good players. There was no

Puskas but they had Bozsik, Sandor, Tichy. These were great players." Webster recalls, "I didn't think we would beat them. They had
such a good reputation. At the time they were up there with Brazil
and West Germany."

Mel Charles was assigned the task of looking after Hungary's
danger-man, the lanky Tichy, who played for Puskas's former club,
Honved. "We were uncertain about Hungary," adds Charles. "They
were runners-up in '54 but the team had changed. Before the game
we would have settled for a draw."

Bowen was told to watch Hidegkuti. Ever since he arrived in Sweden, Murphy had not stopped reminding Bowen of his task against
the illustrious forward. As journalist Jim Hill recalls, "Every time
Murphy saw Bowen, whether it was in the hotel dining-room or outside somewhere, Murphy would shout 'Hidegkuti!' at him. "Everywhere he went there was Murphy shouting 'Dave! Don't forget!
Hidegkuti!'" From the first to the last whistle Bowen kicked the old
and overweight Hungarian. It did the job since Hidegkuti was virtually anonymous. "Hidegkuti never played again after that and Dave
always felt guilty about that match," says Hill.

In the dressing room Murphy gave one of his typical rousing
team-talks. "He was saying, 'Come on boys, give it your best! Don't
let them intimidate you!' He was foaming at the mouth as usual," remembers Webster. "He also told us, 'Tackle hard and make sure it
counts!' That was Murphy's favourite phrase. He used to say it all
the time at United." Webster, like Bowen, had been given a specific
instruction by Murphy. The Wales manager had been alerted to the
threat of Sándor, Hungary's other new star. He was the one player
likely to cause the Welsh defence real problems. Murphy asked his
disciple at United, Webster, to take care of him. "I'll never forget
what he said to me. 'Colin, the first thing you've got to do is to kick
the bastard!' That's what he told me."

The 1958 World Cup was five hours old when the Welsh and
Hungarian players, in front of a 15,342, crowd – it was still 5,000
short of capacity but the organisers were expecting only 8,000 if John
Charles had not been playing – walked out onto the Jernvallen pitch.
Earlier that day, at 2pm, their Group Three rivals Sweden and
Mexico had kicked-off the tournament in Stockholm.

The hosts, in front of a 34,000 crowd including their own King
Gustav, had immediately established themselves as serious contenders with an easy 3–0 victory over the mediocre Mexicans. Agne
Simonsson scored twice, one in each half. Nils Liedholm scored the
third in the second-half, from the penalty spot. That result confirmed
what most people thought of Group Three, that Sweden were dead

certs to progress and that the coveted second place was between Hungary and possibly Wales.

The match at Sandviken, despite being the first for both countries, was now of huge importance. If one of them lost, it would mean the end of their involvement in the World Cup. "Hungary wasn't as good as the team of the early Fifties," says Cliff Jones. "But they still had Hidegkuti, Bozsik and Grosics so we couldn't underestimate them."

The two captains, Bowen and Bozsik, walked over to the centre-circle, exchanged pennants and shook hands. But luck was still evading Wales. They had lost the right to wear red. Now they lost the toss as well. For the Hungarians this was a real advantage. It was a beautiful evening and the sun was low and harsh. Kelsey had noticed the sun would be a hazard for the goalkeeper who had to stare into it. He told Bowen to win the toss and make the Hungarians, and more importantly Grosics, play facing the sun. Bowen, though, came off second best and it was no surprise to see Bozsik tell his players they would start the first-half with their backs to the sun.

Hungary kicked-off and immediately took control, but not before the dutiful Webster obeyed his manager's instructions and made his mark on Sándor. "A ball was coming over towards me and Sándor. It was 60–40 in my favour, but I let it go more for him, then I hit him on the shin and down he went. He got up and started shouting 'You crazy! You crazy!' at me. The funny thing was it hurt me more than it did him and I was the one who needed treatment, not Sándor."

Wales's first World Cup got off to the worst possible start. After barely 240 seconds of football, Bozsik had put the Hungarians in front. Barcs had insisted that Hidegkuti play, despite Baroti's fears. Hidegkuti picked up the ball from midfield and dribbled his way to the edge of the Welsh penalty area. He then squared it to Bozsik, charging up the field in support, who fired the ball past Kelsey from 15 yards. It was a goal chiselled out by the last remnants of the Golden Squad, Hidegkuti and Bozsik.

Losing the toss had been crucial. Kelsey later said he would have stopped Bozsik's shot had he had his back to goal. Instead, with the sun beating down on his face, he struggled to see the ball clearly. "I thought there was going to be an avalanche of goals after that," admits Mel Charles. "I mean, it was a bit of a shock to lose a goal after just four or five minutes." Bozsik should never have been given so much time and space by the Welsh defenders.

Like Mel Charles, the Sandviken crowd were expecting the 1954 finalists to romp home and join Sweden as quarter-finalists. Despite a 20–minute spell of sustained Hungarian pressure, the massacre never materialised. Murphy's men regrouped and, slowly but surely, started to wrestle the game from Hungary. Wales's first chance came after 10 minutes, Allchurch firing wide after combining with Jones.

"I thought the Hungarians would settle down to play," remarked Kelsey. "Instead, they started the rough stuff. John Charles was on the wrong end of some very violent tackling. Every time he got the ball he was tackled by two Hungarian defenders, usually from behind." Charles, the superstar from Serie A, was a marked man. The Hungarians reckoned if they stopped the Gentle Giant, by fair means or foul, that would stop Wales. Within seconds of the start, he was cut down at the ankles by Tichy, the first of a barrage of fouls. They were, however, nothing compared to what the Hungarians would dish out in the play-off, in nine days time.

Ironically, it was the Juventus forward who equalised from a corner after 26 minutes, scoring his country's first goal in the World Cup in the process. "Cliff Jones crossed the ball," recalls Charles, "and I think Colin (Webster) was going to jump for it. I shouted to him 'Leave it!' and he took the centre-half away from me instead so I had a free header." Charles soared above everyone in the area and headed towards Grosics's goal. The Hungarian goalkeeper, who would have a poor World Cup, thought the ball was going wide and made no attempt to save it, but to Charles's delight the ball sneaked inside the post. Wales were deservedly level.

"John bulleted the ball into the net," recalls Cliff Jones. "You could hear the thump as he headed it. It was a real thump. I always hit the ball into a certain area, either on the penalty spot or the far post. That's where John expected me to cross and it worked that night. I never ever crossed to the near post." The winger was causing Mátrai a few problems. "He was one-footed. He wasn't good with his left foot. He wanted me to go inside, so what I'd do is make it look like I was going inside, then when he was about to make his move I'd push the ball outside him."

For the next 19 minutes the Welsh, clearly buoyed by that goal, pushed for a second but the first-half ended 1–1. Despite the Welsh pressure it was the Hungarians who nearly scored a second but Tichy's fierce shot, which flew passed Kelsey, was cleared off the line by Hopkins. Wales kicked-off the second 45 minutes but once again their opponents got off to a better start and nearly retook the lead. Hidegkuti cracked a volley inside the area and it looked a certain goal. Stuart Williams, however, blocked the ball on the line before kicking it to safety.

As the match wore on, it became clear the Hungarians could not get the better of the World Cup debutants. If anything, it was Wales who were looking the more dangerous side. As a result John Charles was receiving some harsh treatment from the worried Hungarian defenders who were quite happy to concede free-kick after free-kick. "They did kick me a lot," says Charles. "I was a marked man right from the whistle and they marked me very, very tightly. They would hold my shirt or pull me down. I remember jumping for a cross and one of the Hungarians put both his hands around my neck."

Charles was not the only victim. Allchurch, too, became a human punchbag and only the remarkable restraint from the Welsh players prevented a brawl. "Hungary's tactics were shocking," said Welsh FA chairman Milwyn Jenkins after the game. "But our boys took it like men – and played magnificently. We might have won had the referee not been a complete stranger to the advantage rule." The Press, which had christened the wonderful side under Puskas as the Mighty Magyars dubbed Baroti's side of 1958 the Mad Magyars for their cynical, often brutal, tackling.

"They were a team on the decline and Hidegkuti wasn't the player he used to be," says Hopkins. "We caught them on a low point in their football history because they came good again in 1966. They had an excellent side then."

In the 72nd minute Wales should have been awarded what might have been a match-winning penalty. Allchurch was clean through and one on one with Grosics, but when he was just six-yards from the Hungarian goal he was tripped from behind by the desperate Mátrai. The entire stadium expected the Uruguayan referee, José Maria Codesal, to award a penalty but incredibly he waved play on, claiming Allchurch had fallen over his own feet. "It may have looked as if I had slipped," the Swansea Town star said after the match, "but you can take it from me that my feet were whipped from under me by Hungarian defenders." Webster remembers the incident clearly. "It looked a blatant penalty but in those days penalties were rarely given. Unlike today, the referees were scared to give them."

The match ended 1–1 and Wales, against all the odds and defying all the pre-match predictions, had snatched a precious point. Group Three had been blown wide open. "Murphy was cock-a-hoop over the result," recalls Webster. "He even thought we should have won the game." John Charles, adds, "Jimmy was jumping around in the dressing room, shouting, 'We'll do it now! We'll go further!' It was a wonderful result for us. He said we should have won and I agree with him. We had more of the match, especially in the second-half."

The Hungarians were heavily criticised after the match, especially two of the survivors from 1954, Grosics, who was blamed for Wales's equaliser, and Hidegkuti, who was a pale, pathetic shadow of the player he was in Switzerland four years earlier. Hidegkuti was no-where to be seen for large chunks of the game.

"It was a small ground at Sandviken and I think that suited us more than the Hungarians," says Charles. "I expected more from Hungary. I was at Wembley when they beat England 6–3 but this was nowhere near the same team." His brother, Mel, also thought Hungary were something of an anti-climax. "They played exactly the same game as us – two fast wingers and a big man up-front."

In 1954 their revolutionary football, arguably the first example of the 4–2–4 system with Puskas, Kocsis, Czibor and Hidegkuti making up the attack, tore opposing defences to shreds. Four years on, they were pretty predictable and the Welsh defenders snuffed out most of their attacks with relative ease.

Afterwards, Baroti put on a brave face and predicted, somewhat optimistically, that the two qualifiers from this group would be his team and Wales, not Sweden. "We were very disappointed to drop a point against Wales," said Hungary's manager, "but they thoroughly deserved to draw. It's no secret we felt dead sure of beating Wales before the kick-off and it was a tremendous shock to us to see the way they played." As for a satisfied Murphy, he said, "It was a good result to a hard game, but we should have had the penalty. It should always be a penalty when a player is charged in the back in the penalty area."

Stanley Rous, FIFA commissar for the Hungary-Wales match, said afterwards, "Wales put up a wonderful performance. When you lack individual skill in certain positions you have to find a substitute. Wales have done that. They have the fighting fervour."

Williams, who made that crucial goal-line clearance in the second-half, remarks, "A draw was a fair result. It was a tight game and we were evenly matched. Hungary had some good players but not the outstanding players they had in 1954. We had a hard core of world-class players in our 16 and they were all in the right positions – Kelsey in goal, Allchurch in the middle, Cliff on the wing and John up front. We also had great team spirit."

Webster, whose experimental combination with Medwin on the right did not really work, says, "We held our own. At times we were better. We thought at the time even if we did go out at the first stage then at least we had the satisfaction of playing well against Hungary."

In the stand the seven Welsh players not selected for the game sat and watched their team-mates match Hungary man for man. One of the seven, Hewitt, remarks, "The players were relaxed.

There was no tension at all. If anything we were too relaxed which is why Hungary scored first. They thought they were going to murder us but it was clear soon after the kick-off that they were no better than us."

Codesal was roundly condemned for refusing to award what was a clear-cut penalty. For Murphy's side, there was nothing but praise. When, on June 2, they had arrived in Stockholm, they were held up as condemned men, cannon fodder, a team lucky to be in Sweden. But now they could sniff the quarter-finals. "I was satisfied with the 1–1 draw," admits Cliff Jones. "Some people say we should have won but we were pleased with that result."

Sweden's manager, Raynor, was one of the faces in the crowd. As soon as the Russian referee Nikolai Latychev blew the whistle on the Sweden-Mexico match in Stockholm earlier that afternoon the Yorkshireman had jumped into his car and made the 125-mile trip to Sandviken to run the rule over his side's next two opponents. It was Wales, not Hungary, who now worried him. The Welsh defence had played superbly and their counter-attacks, although infrequent, were dangerous. "England and Wales play the power game," Raynor said after the 1–1 draw. "By comparison with this match, ours was like a ballet dance. Frankly, we thought the Hungarians were our only worry. Now we have got them and Wales on our plate."

The Swedish press, who also assumed Hungary were the only threat to the host nation topping Group Three, had also taken notice. "But now we have two great soccer powers to beat," commented the *Dagens Nyheter* newspaper the following day, while the headline in *Tioningen*, a Stockholm daily, read 'John Charles Was Gigantic'. Charles, from whom so much was expected in Sweden, would have a mixed time in the 1958 World Cup. For the Juventus striker there would be much heartbreak later on. This, the opening match against Hungary, would be one of his few high points.

Surprise though it was, Wales's draw with the 1954 finalists was not the biggest shock of the opening day. That occurred in Group One, in the Örjans Vall stadium in Halmstad where nearly 11,000 people watched Northern Ireland beat the tournament's dark horses, Czechoslovakia, by a single goal. It came after 21 minutes, Wilbur Cush heading home a Peter McParland cross past the helpless Czech goalkeeper Dolejsi. The Irish, particularly their outstanding goalkeeper, Gregg, survived sustained Czech pressure in the second-half to record a memorable, and unexpected, victory.

West Germany, the holders, also started well, beating the fancied Argentinians 3–1 in Malmö in the other Group One match. The South Americans started well and Creste Corbatta put them in front after three minutes but the Germans went into the interval 2–1 up thanks to goals from Uwe Seeler, in his first ever World Cup match, and Helmut Rahn. In the second-half Rahn bagged his second of the game, a curving shot a minute from time. Argentina without Sivori, Maschio and Angelillo were, as feared, a mere shadow of the team that won the 1957 Copa America in such emphatic style. It worried manager Stàbile that Argentina failed to make an impact, even though the Germans, who were carrying a limping Horst Eckel, their right-half, were effectively down to 10 men for most of the second-half.

In Group Two, the Scots and the Yugoslavs had to settle for a goal apiece and a point apiece. In the Arosvallen stadium in Västeras, the managerless Scots were given an early fright when Aleksandar Petakovic gave Yugoslavia the lead after six minutes. Scotland spent the first 45 minutes fighting for survival. In the second-half, Jimmy Murray headed Scotland's equaliser just seconds after Petakovic hit the post at the other end.

The remaining Group Two sides, France and Paraguay, met in Norrköping's Idrottsparken, the venue for the first hammering of the 1958 competition. France won an extraordinary game 7–3. Amazingly, it was Paraguay who took the lead with a goal from Florencio Amarilla after 20 minutes. Just Fontaine then put France in front with two goals before Amarilla, in the 45th minute, scored from the penalty spot to make it 2–2. After the break the see-saw continued with Jorgelino Romero putting Paraguay back in front after 50 minutes. But after that it was all France. Roger Piantoni made it 3–3 just two minutes after Romero's goal and the Paraguayans capitulated. Marian Wisnieski made it 4–3 after 61 minutes and Fontaine completed his hat-trick in the 67th minute to make it 5–3. A minute later Raymond Kopa scored France's sixth before Jean Vincent completed the rout six minutes from time. After this performance, the French were installed as one of the favourites to lift the Jules Rimet Trophy.

In Group Four, the Brazilians easily dispatched Austria 3–0 in the Rimnersvallen stadium in Uddevalla. Mazzola, whose real name was José Altafini (he was nicknamed Mazzola because of his likeness to the great Torino and Italy captain Valentino Mazzola, who died in the Superga air crash in 1949), scored after 39 and 89 minutes with Nilton Santos scoring in-between, after 49 minutes.

As for England, they drew 2–2 with the Soviet Union in Gothenburg, in a dramatic match played under the Ullevi Stadium's futuristic wire-suspended roof. Nikita Simonian put the Soviets in front after goalkeeper Colin McDonald could only parry Alex Ivanov's low shot. And it was Ivanov who put the Soviets 2–0 up 11 minutes into the second-half, rounding the Fulham goalkeeper and poking home what seemed a killer second goal. After that the English fought back. Derek Kevan rose above the Russian defence to make it 2–1. Bobby Robson then thought he had made it 2–2 but the referee, Istvan Zsolt of Hungary, blew for a foul by Kevan on Yashin.

Zsolt was again involved in controversy five minutes from time when he awarded England a lifesaving penalty. Johnny Haynes was brought down but the Russians protested it was outside the area. Zsolt stood his ground and Tom Finney, with his last ever World Cup kick, made it 2–2.

The first day of the 1958 tournament had come and gone. Group One, after Northern Ireland's shock win and Argentina's equally shocking demise, was impossible to call. France had taken control of Group Two with Scotland and Yugoslavia battling to join them in the last eight. In Group Three, Sweden lived up to their billing but Wales, after their draw with fading Hungary, now had a fine chance of reaching the quarter-finals. And in Group Four the question already being asked was, who will join Brazil in the next round, England or the Soviet Union?

CHAPTER EIGHT

THE MEXICO DEBACLE

THE Welsh team, following the draw with Hungary, arrived back at the Grand Hotel at 2am the following morning. The players were so drained by the intensity of the event they were unable to raise their voices and sing during the bus journey back to their hotel in Soltsjöbaden.

It had been a physical contest and later that morning, after allowing his squad a well-deserved lie-in, Jimmy Murphy and trainer Jack Jones went through the 11 who had played in Sandviken to treat any casualties. It was unlikely any player injured against the Hungarians would figure in the next match, against Mexico in Stockholm. The next phase of first-round matches was scheduled for June 11 – just two days away.

Murphy and Jones found two walking wounded and they were both defenders – Mel Hopkins, who was suffering with a grazed hip, and Derrick Sullivan, who had injured his left knee. The news regarding Sullivan was the most worrying for Murphy. The Cardiff City defender missed nine internationals during the 1957/58 season following a cartilage operation on the same knee. Murphy and Jones looked at it closely. It had swollen badly overnight so Vic Crowe and Colin Baker were put on stand-by.

Mexico, along with Wales and Northern Ireland, were considered one of the weakest teams in Sweden, but while the two British teams had distinguished themselves in the opening game, and perhaps shed their pushover tags, the Mexicans had not. In that first match of the competition, against Sweden in Stockholm, they played dreadfully and were lucky to escape with a 3–0 beating. Karl Svensson, Sweden's goalkeeper, had so little to do against the feeble Mexican attack that he might just as well have left the pitch and joined the crowd watching from the Rasunda Stadium's stands.

Little was known about this Mexico team although the fact their players were on a £100–a-man winning bonus, an incentive which stunned Murphy's players who had no such agreement, spread throughout the country like wildfire. Cynics no doubt observed that if the performance against Sweden was anything to go by there was little chance of the Mexican FA having to pay out any bonus. In Sweden, the Welsh players received £50, the normal rate for playing for their country, while those who were not picked to play received £35.

The Mexicans were hardly World Cup novices. This may have been the first tournament for Wales, but it was Mexico's fourth. Their World Cup record, though, was nothing to write home about. The Mexicans had lost every one of the nine World Cup games they had played. In 1930 they lost all three of their matches to France, Chile and Argentina. It was the same story in 1950, losing this time to Brazil, Yugoslavia and Switzerland and in 1954 they lost again to Brazil and France. In the first match of 1958, against Sweden, nothing had changed. In those nine games the Mexicans had conceded no less than 34 goals.

They may well have qualified for their third consecutive World Cup, but their qualifying group, the Central and North American Zone, was considered one of the weakest qualifying sections of all. Mexico had topped Group Two ahead of Canada and the USA before beating the winners of Group One, Costa Rica, in the decisive two-leg play-off match. They beat the Costa Ricans 2–1 in Mexico and drew 1–1 away.

Morale among the Mexican squad was already low when they arrived in Stockholm. En route they had played two warm-up matches in Portugal, against Benfica and Sporting Lisbon, and lost both 3–0 and 2–0 respectively. After the heavy defeat against the host nation, morale was non-existent.

The Welsh team were boosted by reports from British journalists who had visited the Mexican camp at Bosön, high in the forest and 30 miles from Stockholm. There, journalists were stunned by the funereal atmosphere at their base. The Mexican players seemed more interested in playing tennis on the Idrottsinstitutet's impressive courts than warming-up for their do-or-die match with the Welsh. A so-called training session amounted to a few reserve players lazily kicking a ball at goalkeeper Antonio Carbajal who, incidentally, was starring in his third World Cup. The outside-right, Alfredo Garcia, a cheerful figure who played his mouth-organ before the Sweden match, was now silent and depressed. The rest of the Mexican squad were inside the hotel listening to records while their manager, Antonio Lopez, was locked away in his room, thinking of how to avoid another bad defeat.

Lopez had problems. For the Wales match he looked set to lose his two full-backs through injury, Jesus Del Muro and José Villegas. Small wonder, then, that Wales were overwhelming favourites to beat Mexico in the concrete bowl that was Stockholm's Rasunda Stadium, on June 11. What a difference a single match made. Few, if anyone, gave Wales a chance of winning one of their three first-round matches. Now, on the back of their impressive performance against Hungary and Mexico's dire display against Sweden, a Welsh win was a formality.

Even Sweden's manager had joined the bandwagon predicting a straightforward victory for Murphy's men. "Wales should beat Mexico easily," said Raynor, the day before the match. "The Mexicans are fast and pretty but they keep their half-backs too far forward and they play across the field without getting anywhere. Wales on the other hand keep moving forward and make the ball do the work."

The condition of the pitch in the Rasunda Stadium, situated in Solna, a municipality north of Stockholm, also favoured the Welsh. Before the Hungary game, Murphy, believing a soft pitch would be an advantage for his team, prayed for rain. It never really came, despite the occasional shower. But after the Hungary match the heavens opened and Stockholm was hit by thunderstorms. Murphy was delighted. The pretty passing of the Mexican game would surely come unstuck on a heavy pitch while Wales's physical and more direct style would be unaffected.

But Murphy, with talk about how Wales would sweep aside the allegedly unhappy Mexicans, was beginning to worry about complacency among his squad. He was especially annoyed at Raynor's pre-match comments. "I'm not being kidded by talk of the Mexicans being a team of ballet dancers," said Murphy. "My boys will be told to give everything they've got. If we bag the goals, as many as people have told me we will, then all the better."

Murphy kept the door open for Sullivan for as long as possible but on the night of June 10 it was announced the Cardiff City defender had not responded to treatment and was not fit to play. "You can rest assured that Sullivan will not play unless he is 100 per cent fit," explained Murphy. "We will not jeopardise his career for anything."

The news about right-half Sullivan was quite a blow for Murphy. Although Sullivan was not one of the squad's international stars he had been outstanding in the first match. Now the Welsh manager was forced to disturb the defence which had so impressively kept the Hungarian forwards at bay. In the end the nod went to Colin Baker,

Welsh team manager Jimmy Murphy discusses tactics with some of his squad in March 1957, two months before Wales's first World Cup qualifying match against Czechoslovakia.

Vlastimil Bubnik hits the post during the Wales-Czechoslovakia match at Cardiff.

Welsh defender Mel Charles, Ron Stitfall and Mel Hopkins watch goalkeeper Jack Kelsey save a Czech effort.

Wales line up in front of 110,000 people in Leipzig's Zentralstadion for the second qualifying match against East Germany. Left to right: M. Charles, Hopkins, Vernon, Medwin, Jones, Harris, Tapscott, Edwards, Kelsey, J. Charles.
(Courtesy of Mel Hopkins)

Wales go 2-0 up against East Germany in Cardiff. Goalkeeper Gunther Busch (centre) punches a Cliff Jones cross into his own net.

Terry Medwin shoots wide during Wales's 2-0 win over Israel in the first World Cup play-off in Tel Aviv. Gideon Tisch is the Israeli defender in the way.

Shoshana Ahud, an Israeli student in London, presents the Welsh squad with oranges before the second play-off in Cardiff. Left to right. Stuart Williams, Mel Hopkins, Jimmy Murphy, Mel Charles, Ron Hewitt and Dave Bowen.

The Welsh team which beat Israel 2-0 in Cardiff. Back row, left to right: Harrington, Williams, J. Charles, Kelsey, Hopkins, Allchurch, M. Charles, Medwin, Hewitt, Bowen, Jones.

John Charles and Israeli goalkeeper Yaacov Chodoroff jump for a high ball. Chodoroff suffered concussion, a broken nose and a sprained shoulder in the challenge with Charles.

Ivor Allchurch scores the first goal against the Israelis. Terry Medwin (far left) looks on.

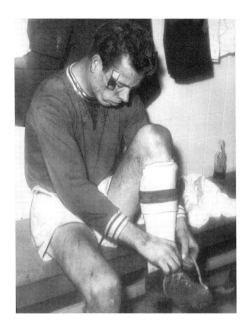

Welsh football's personae non gratae. Derek Tapscott (top left), Ray Daniel (top right) and Trevor Ford (bottom) were all excluded from the Welsh squad that flew to Sweden.

World Cup warm-up in London's Hyde Park. Manager
Jimmy Murphy (centre) makes a point to Dave Bowen (left)
and Cliff Jones.

The Welsh party, minus John Charles, arrive at Stockholm's Bromma
Airport on June 2, 1958. Holding the bouquet of flowers is Milwyn
Jenkins, chairman of the Welsh FA.

The luxurious Grand Hotel in Soltsjöbaden, where the Welsh squad stayed for the first-round matches. *(Courtesy of Colin Baker)*

Wales's captain Dave Bowen and manager Jimmy Murphy meet Swedish captain and AC Milan star Nils Liedholm before Sweden's warm-up match in Gustavsberg on June 3.

The Welsh contingent pose outside the Grand Hotel. Left to right: Jack Jones (trainer), Mel Charles, Ivor Allchurch, John Charles, Cliff Jones, Roy Vernon, Jimmy Murphy (manager), Mel Hopkins, Jack Kelsey, Vic Crowe, Trevor Edwards, Ron Hewitt, Dave Bowen.*(Courtesy of Mel Hopkins)*

John Charles rises above the Hungarian defence to score Wales's 26th minute equaliser against Hungary in Sandviken.
(Associated Press)

Mexican players mob goalscorer Jaime Belmonte after his last-minute equaliser against Wales in Stockholm. The Welsh player on the floor is Mel Hopkins. *(Associated Press)*

Jack Kelsey catches a high ball during the Sweden-Wales match in Stockholm. The Arsenal goalkeeper was in inspired form as Wales earned the 0-0 draw which kept their World Cup dream alive. *(Courtesy of the Welsh FA)*

Sweden goalkeeper Karl Svensson saves from Roy Vernon during a rare Welsh attack.

Ron Hewitt beats Hungary's Mate Fenyvesi to the ball in the first-round play-off match in Stockholm. *(Courtesy of Ron Hewitt)*

Gyula Groscis, the famous Hungarian goalkeeper, turns around to see Ivor Allchurch's 25 yard shot hit the back of the net. It was one of the best goals of the 1958 World Cup.*(Associated Press)*

The goal that put Wales into the quarter-finals. Terry Medwin slots the ball past Gyula Groscis. A crowd of only 2,823 saw Wales's first and, so far, only win in the World Cup.

Cliff Jones outjumps his marker De Sordi in the quarter final against Brazil in Gothenburg.

Jack Kelsey, chewing gum rubbed into his hands, stops yet another Brazilian attack.

Pelé playing his second World Cup match, is thwarted by Jack Kelsey.
José Altafini looks on.

Jack Kelsey beats José Altafini to the ball. Mel Hopkins and Stuart Williams are
the two defenders on the line.

The goal that knocked Wales out of the World Cup. Pelé toe-pokes the ball past Jack Kelsey. *(Associated Press)*

The Brazilian players pile on top of Pelé inside the Welsh goal seconds after his 73rd minute winner. Mel Hopkins (dark socks) tries to retrieve the ball. *(Associated Press)*

The right-back. Stuart Williams, one of the outstanding defenders of the 1958 tournament.

The outside-right. Terry Medwin, scorer of the play-off winner against Hungary.

The left-back. Mel Hopkins, with a souvenir from Wales's Swedish adventure.

The centre-half, Mel Charles, who made the 1958 World Cup XI.

The inside-right. Ron Hewitt, whose last game for Wales was the quarter-final against Brazil.

The centre-forward. John Charles, scorer of Wales's first ever World Cup goal.

Ken Jones, understudy to Jack Kelsey, was one of the four players who did not get a World Cup game.

Colin Webster was dropped after the Mexico game, but replaced the injured John Charles for the quarter-final.

The outside-right. Cliff Jones, who, by his own admission, had a disappointing World Cup.

Colin Baker made one appearance in Sweden, against Mexico.

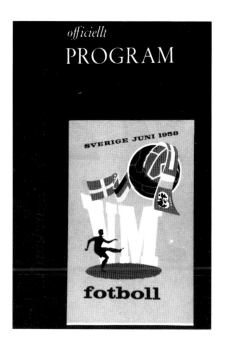

(Top) The official programme for the Wales v. Brazil
quarter-final on 19 June 1958.

(Bottom) An English-language guide to the
1958 World Cup tournament.

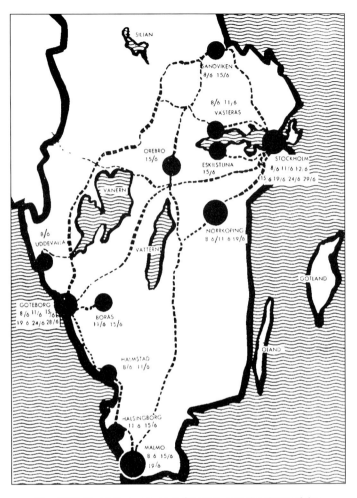

SILJAN

SANDVIKEN
8/6 15/6

8/6 11/6
VASTERAS

OREBRO
15/6

ESKILSTUNA
15/6

STOCKHOLM
8/6 11/6 12/6
15/6 19/6 24/6 29/6

VANERN

NORRKOPING
8/6/11/6 19/6

8/6
UDDEVALLA

VATTERN

GOTLAND

GOTEBORG
8/6 11/6 15/6
19/6 24/6 28/6

BORAS
11/6 15/6

OLAND

HALMSTAD
8/6 11/6

HALSINGBORG
11/6 15/6

MALMO
8/6 15/6
19/6

The 1958 World Cup venues in Sweden, with the dates of the
games played at each location.

a team-mate of Sullivan's at Ninian Park, a star in Wales's victory over England in the under-23 match at Wrexham and the quietest member of 'the Big Five'. Baker, though, had never played for Wales at senior level.

"There were no subs in those days and I didn't expect to play," recalls Baker. His customary role was left-half but being two-footed he could also play right-half with equal aplomb. "I thought I was there just to make up the numbers. I was nervous to start off with but I soon got into the game. We had some good players, terrific players in fact – John Charles, Jack Kelsey, Ivor Allchurch. In my opinion it was the best side Wales has ever had. It was wonderful to be a part of it."

Sadly for Baker, the Mexico match would not be the happiest of debuts since what followed was one of the most disappointing performances given by a Welsh international team. The line-up for the match read: Kelsey, Williams, Hopkins, Baker, Mel Charles, Bowen, Webster, Medwin, John Charles, Allchurch, Jones. Murphy had decided to persist with the much-maligned combination of Medwin and Webster on the right.

The kick-off time for the Wales-Mexico match was once again 7pm. All first-round matches started at 7pm except two involving Sweden – the first against the Mexicans and the last against the Welsh – which both had a 2pm kick-off.

Lopez, not surprisingly, wielded the axe and made five changes from the team which was swept aside by the Swedes in the same stadium three days earlier. In defence Miguel Gutiérrez replaced the injured José Villegas and Raul Cardenas replaced Alfonso Portugal. In attack Jaime Belmonte came in for Hector Hernández, Carlos Blanco for Carlos Calderon while Carlos González replaced winger Gutiérrez who was moved to left-back. There was some good news for the troubled Lopez. Del Muro, the full-back injured against the Swedes, was declared fit.

In the Welsh dressing room Murphy gave another of his famous, and undiplomatic, team-talks. As John Charles recalls, "He stood in the middle of the room and told us 'These people, they can't even play football!' He was calling the Mexicans 'ranchos' and said they were only good for riding horses, not playing football." Murphy had seen the Mexicans in their first match against Sweden and was not impressed. "He came back from that game and said to us, 'We can beat these! This lot are rubbish!' But we didn't know anything about them except that being from Latin America they would be good with the ball," says Charles.

Murphy knew victory against Mexico would put the pressure on

Sweden and Hungary who were playing their match the following day, in Stockholm.

A crowd of more than 15,000, most of them Swedes – although there were a few hundred loud travelling Mexicans as well – was inside the Rasunda Stadium for this one, and just about everyone was cheering for Mexico. Not only were they the underdogs but defeat for Wales would mean Sweden would be virtually guaranteed a place in the quarter-finals.

"We came out onto the pitch and saw all these people wearing sombreros," says Mel Charles. "All you could hear was 'Messico! Messico! Messico!' There was hardly anyone cheering for us (there were a couple of hundred Royal Navy seamen who had stopped overnight in Stockholm). We had about 100 fans, that's all, but they had a hell of a lot of support. It doesn't really affect players, though. Once a game gets going you don't notice the crowd."

Just 10 minutes after kick-off and it was clear this was not the same Welsh performance which had startled Hungary in Sandviken. This one was careless, listless and ragged. Nevertheless, Wales, again playing into the sun, snatched the lead after 33 minutes through 'Golden Boy' Ivor Allchurch. Like the Welsh performance, the goal was hardly vintage. From a Colin Webster corner on the right, Allchurch volleyed towards Carbajal's goal, but instead of connecting sweetly he more or less mis-hit the ball. Still, there was enough power for it to sneak past the Mexican goalkeeper. 1–0 to Wales.

It was a lead they did not deserve. Mexico, in their green shirts, had played some fine football and their crisp passing was causing Wales problems. Twice in the opening 15 minutes Francisco Flores threatened Kelsey's goal, first with a low shot and then with a header. Baker, though, did hit the post. The young defender almost capped his debut with a goal, beating off two defenders before chipping past the bewildered Carbajal but the ball grazed the upright.

After Allchurch's goal Wales were expected to settle down, improve and perhaps score more goals. The Welsh players remembered what a bunch of travelling Mexican supporters staying in the Grand Hotel told them before the game. If Wales managed to score one, they would go on to score a hatful. Mexico never reacted well to conceding the first goal.

Wales were unable to increase their lead and neither, thanks mainly to Webster's robust tackling, did they endear themselves to the 15,150 crowd. One particular challenge, on Gutiérrez, incensed the Mexican fans and two of them jumped onto the pitch and chased the Manchester United player down the touchline. "It was a 50–50 ball and I went in hard and the full-back stayed down," says

Webster. The challenge occurred right in front of the Mexican supporters. "They were shouting at me and a few of them threw their
sombreros at me. A couple of them even came onto the pitch to grab
hold of me, but they were stopped by officials before they could catch
me. It wasn't the first time someone has come onto the pitch and
chased after me," smiles Webster. "During a reserve match at
Barnsley with United this old man with a walking stick chased after
me claiming I had fouled one of the Barnsley lads."

After that almost comical episode Webster and Terry Medwin –
for Webster's own safety – swapped positions. Medwin went outside-
right while Webster moved inside-right. "We decided to get Colin
out of it for 10 to 15 minutes," recalls Medwin. "The thing with Colin
was he wouldn't let things lie. If someone kicked him he made sure he
got them back." When the Yugoslav referee, Leo Lemesic, restarted
the match, Webster and the rest of the Welsh team were jeered and
booed every time they touched the ball.

"I tackled the Mexican like I always did – hard," says Webster.
"I'd go in with my shoulder. As far as I was concerned it wasn't a bad
challenge and the referee didn't book me. The Mexican was overact-
ing. They played differently to us. They were good with the ball but
they couldn't take the hits like a British player. Every time we
touched them they would fall down and cry."

John Charles says Murphy later admonished Webster for his
over-aggressive approach to the match. For the third game, against
Sweden, Webster was dropped from the team. "He played hell with
Colin for charging round the way he did," says Charles. "Jimmy said
if we tackled like that all the time we'd get a bad name. Against
Mexico we were the villains because of some of the tackles that were
flying about."

The animosity between the Welsh and the Mexicans was not con-
fined to the pitch. In the stands, Ken Jones, Wales's reserve goalkeeper, nearly got involved in a brawl with Mexico's reserve players.
"They were having a go at us, recalls Jones. "They knew who we were
because the reserves had to wear their blazers to the matches. They
were looking at us and laughing. I didn't understand what they were
saying but I could tell they were trying to wind us up, so I gave them
two fingers." The Mexicans did not take kindly to that gesture and
squared up to the Cardiff City goalkeeper. "There was some aggro
out on the pitch and it spilled into the stands. Every time there was a
hard challenge on one of the Mexicans the reserves would have a go
at us and they were sitting just inches from us. We would have a go
back, shouting 'Viva Zapata!' and calling them 'Bloody Mexies'. It
was just a little bit of banter which got out of hand." Murphy, from

the touchline down below, had noticed the fracas involving Jones. "He sent Jack Jones to come and get me. I had to sit on the bench next to Murphy for the rest of the game. Every so often, he would put his hand in his pocket to take out his little flask of whisky for a swig. He loved his whisky, Murphy. He could drink whisky for breakfast, that man."

At the interval Wales were still leading 1–0. Murphy, unhappy with the first 45 minutes, tried to raise his team for the second-half. Without a two-goal cushion the threat of Mexico grabbing an equaliser, and a share of the points, was very real. The break appeared to do Wales no good at all. They were as bad in the second-half as they were in the first. Mexico's centre-half Jorge Romo was marking John Charles out of the game while Cliff Jones, constantly slipping on the wet, greasy surface, rarely got the better of Del Muro. Hewitt, who relished playing on a soft pitch, had been ignored by Murphy who persisted with Webster at inside-right.

Mervyn Thomas, football correspondent for the *South Wales Echo*, was one of the observers shocked by his country's awful display. "I have seen Wales play some bad internationals," he wrote. "This time they were so downright disappointing that few of them deserve one halfpenny of the £50 they each picked up for playing. In fact, I have suggested to them that they should donate their fees to some worthy charity."

The Mexicans, far from being the pushover ballet dancers, were proving difficult to break down. Wales were not playing well. "Such was their fitness," said Kelsey later, "that they attacked with 10 men and defended with 10 men. Every man in the side appeared to be a ball player and we simply couldn't make any headway." Wales now realised the effect over-confidence can have on a team. Three days before, the Hungarians had anticipated cruising to victory against the Welsh and they paid the penalty for their arrogance.

Wales protected the lead until the 89th minute. Then, with Baker lying on the touchline having treatment for cramp, the Mexicans broke clear. Outside-left Enrique Sesma crossed and the unmarked Jaime Belmonte, one of the five new faces introduced by Lopez, dived in to head Mexico's equaliser passed the stranded Kelsey, who had no chance of saving it. Belmonte, the inside-right, had missed a good chance earlier in the game. Now all was forgiven. The Mexicans were delirious with joy. Every one of them was inside Wales's six-yard box hugging Belmonte. Even Carbajal sprinted from his goalmouth to congratulate the forward.

Wales quickly restarted but there was barely 90 seconds left to snatch the winner. Having failed to find a second goal for an hour there was no way they were going to find it in a minute-and-a-half. "I remember the ball running out of play by the Welsh bench," says John Charles. "Jimmy picked the ball up, put it under his jumper and pretended he was walking out of the ground. That was his way of showing how unhappy he was with us." Charles, the hero against Hungary, had had a nightmare against Mexico. His contribution amounted to four harmless headers, although the service he received from the wingers was pretty poor.

When Lemesic blew the whistle he ended one of Wales's worst performances since the war. Murphy's men trudged back to the dressing room. At 7.30pm, their future in the competition had seemed assured. Ninety minutes later, it was hanging in the balance. For Lopez and the Mexicans, it was celebration time. If they could get the right result against Hungary, they would progress.

"Jimmy wasn't very pleased with us at the end," adds Charles. "He went into a corner and started muttering, 'You're bloody rubbish!' and, 'That was terrible!' I didn't think a draw was that bad. As long as we didn't lose it was all right. We weren't too disappointed. It was a reasonable result and there was another match to go. We didn't play well. It was just one of those days. They weren't the best team in the world and maybe we went down to their level. But credit to the Mexicans, their passing and ball control were good."

Wales had let slip the perfect opportunity to take charge of Group Three. With Sweden, one of the strongest teams in the tournament, as their next opponents, and with Hungary having the easier task against Mexico, it looked like Murphy and his players would soon be packing their bags. The selectors certainly thought so. When they initially booked their flight to Stockholm they left the return date open. Now, following the Mexico match, they had booked a flight back to London after the Sweden match on June 15.

"We should have hammered Mexico," says Webster. "We were a better side. We just couldn't put the ball in the net. I think if we had a penalty that day we would've missed it. It was just one of those things. That's always been Wales's trouble. We don't win the games we should win."

Cliff Jones, who was expected to unsettle defences in Sweden, played poorly on the left-wing while once again the Webster-Medwin combination hardly set the world alight. "We got a draw so it wasn't a complete disaster," says Jones. "The trend of no easy games started in that World Cup. I didn't have a good game. I had an off-day. I was trying to do too much and ran into trouble." Hopkins, a player Jones would link up with at Tottenham after the World Cup, says, "Mexico played better than we expected. Perhaps we were too confident. As the match went on we were doing silly things and the Mexicans gained confidence from that. Considering the hard work we put in against Hungary this was a low point. The expectations were so high. After we scored one everybody thought we'd get three or four, but it doesn't work out like that."

As for John Charles, who was expected to score a bagful against the fragile Mexican defence, the Juventus striker had no opportunity to prove his worth. "We just couldn't get that killer second goal," says Medwin. "I think we also took Mexico for granted. It was a shame because if we had won we would have been in the driving seat in our group."

After the game the players were accused of complacency, of believing the pre-match hype and playing as if they would be given the two points just for turning up. Stuart Williams, however, denies any over-confidence in the Welsh camp. "Yes, we were expected to win and yes, we didn't play well, but it wasn't down to complacency. It was just one of those days. We just didn't get going. A draw was about as much as we deserved. I don't know what went wrong, but Mexico played well. They could keep possession although they were limited when it came to finishing."

Mel Charles believes Mexico, who were reputed to be the weakest team in the 1958 competition, were not as bad as the critics, and even the Mexican supporters, had made them out to be. "They had some good individuals and on the whole they weren't a bad team. They were small, quick and very tricky."

The Press back home were highly critical of the Welsh display. 'NO ALIBIS FOR WALES. EVEN CHARLES FLOPPED AGAINST FIGHTING MEXICANS' was the headline in the *South Wales Echo*. The *Western Mail* was even more savage. 'WELSH DISPLAY WAS SHOCKING. DRAW WITH MEXICO MAY MEAN EXIT FROM EVENT'. In 48 hours Murphy's men had gone from national heroes to national villains.

Hewitt, who once more watched from the stand, claims Mexico, after their 3–0 drubbing against the Swedes, raised their game against the Welsh as a matter of pride. "They set their stall out right from the start. They kept the ball and didn't mind not scoring. They would make six passes across the back. They had lost heavily against Sweden and I think that made them more cautious. Murphy didn't say too much to us after the game. When he didn't say anything that was a sign he wasn't happy with us. Jimmy would praise us if we played well. But after this one he hardly said a word.

"There were no easy games in that World Cup," adds Hewitt. "Mexico had qualified. They were there. It was 11 against 11, but it was sickening to concede a goal in the last minute. Everyone was asleep when that Mexican scored. The Press had a go about us the next day but that did us the world of good. We didn't play another bad game after that."

It was a disappointing result for Wales but the next day Sweden did them a massive favour by beating Hungary 2–1. Following Hungary's rough tactics against Wales the Swedish FA were anticipating crowd trouble and 200 stewards and 110 police were brought into the Rasunda Stadium to deal with any problems from the traditionally subdued Swedish audience. No trouble arose. Baroti dropped the disappointing Hidegkuti and moved Bozsik to centre-forward in the hope of spicing the attack, but the move did not work.

Kurt Hamrin, Sweden's brilliant right-winger, scored both goals, the first after 34 minutes and the second, with the aid of a lucky deflection, after 56 minutes. A minute before Sweden's second goal Tichy, Hungary's best player, saw a shot hit the Swedish bar. Tichy scored from a great strike in the 77th minute but the Hungarians, unimpressive for the second consecutive game, were unable to find the equaliser. This result meant Sweden, on four points, were guaranteed a place in the last eight. Wales were in second-place and had to at least draw with Sweden to be sure of a play-off against Mexico or Hungary.

In Group One another miracle was beyond Northern Ireland who fell 3–1 to Argentina in Halmstad. A sensation was again on the cards when McParland scored after three minutes, but seven minutes from the interval Dick Keith handled in the area and Swedish referee Sten Ahlner had no hesitation in awarding a penalty which Corbatta duly converted. Argentina, who needed a win to keep their World Cup hopes alive, dominated the second-half and Norberto Menendez and Ludovico Avio put the match beyond the plucky Irish.

Czechoslovakia and West Germany fought out an entertaining 2–2 draw in Halsingborg. The Czechs raced into a 2–0 first-half lead with goals from Milan Dvorak, from the penalty spot, and Zdenek Zikan. But even in 1958 the Germans were masters of the comeback. In the 1954 final they came from 2 0 down against Hungary to win 3–2. Now they would give the Czechs a scare. Hans Schäfer scored on the hour and Helmut Rahn hit his third goal of the competition with 20 minutes remaining. West Germany now topped the group with three points, Northern Ireland and Argentina had two and Czechoslovakia one.

In Group Two, there was disaster for Scotland who lost 3–2 against Paraguay in Norrköping. The Paraguayans, who conceded seven against France, brought in a new goalkeeper, Samuel Aguilar, who replaced the shell-shocked Ramon Mageregger. As for Scotland they were without left-back John Hewie, winger Stuart Imlach and inside-right Jimmy Murray. All three were injured against Yugoslavia. Paraguay scored first, from Juan Aguero after just four minutes. Jackie Mudie levelled the scores 20 minutes later, but the turning point came on the stroke of half-time when Cayetano Re put Paraguay back in front. José Parodi made it three with 19 minutes left. A minute later Bobby Collins made it 3–2 but after that Scotland had nothing left in the tank.

In the other Group Two match, Fontaine brought his World Cup tally to five with two further goals against Yugoslavia, but his double strike could not save the French from a 3–2 defeat in Västeras. Fontaine netted first after four minutes before Petakovic equalised 10 minutes later. Todor Veselinovic put the Yugoslavs ahead in the 61st minute although Fontaine looked to have sealed a draw with a strike five minutes from the end. However, Veselinovic scored the winner, and his second, in the dying seconds to put Yugoslavia top of the table with three points. France and Paraguay were second with two points while things were looking bleak for Scotland, who had one point and free-scoring France left to play.

In Group Four, there was more misery for the Austrians who, despite making seven changes to the team that lost to Brazil, fell 2–0 to the Soviet Union. The Russians, still without their key player, Igor Netto, made easy work of Austria who were badly missing their Italian-based player, Ocwirk. Anatoli Ilyin opened the scoring after quarter of an hour and Ivanov made the match safe in the 62nd minute. The Austrians, who finished third in the 1954 tournament, became the first team to be eliminated from the 1958 series.

The big match of the first-round took place in Gothenburg where Brazil met England. In 1956, at Wembley, England beat the Brazilians 4–2. This time it ended 0–0 with the Brazilians having slightly more of the play. At the England camp before the match, the talk was not about who would mark Didi or how they would breach the iron-strong Brazilian defence, but what was going on between England captain Billy Wright and Joy Beverley. The day before the Brazil game, Fleet Street had revealed Wright's romantic affair with the eldest of the singing trio, the Beverley Sisters. It did not affect the Wolves star who was one of England's best players against the South Americans.

England were without Finney, who would miss the rest of the tournament with a torn muscle. He was replaced by Liverpool's Alan

A'Court. McDonald was superb in goal, Mazzola hit the post and Vavà hit the bar. England, too, had their chances but Haynes, Robson and Kevan failed to capitalise. Brazil had appeared in every World Cup since 1930. This was the first time they had failed to score. After two games Brazil and the Soviet Union were on three points, England two and poor Austria the only team with nothing.

CHAPTER NINE

'WE'RE NOT PLAYBOYS'

FOR the first time since arriving in Soltsjöbaden a sense of unease had penetrated the once jovial Welsh camp. The unanimous criticism of their performance against Mexico, the worst performance under Murphy's reign and arguably the worst since the war, had affected the players. Fleet Street and the Welsh media had turned on them. No longer were they spirited no-hopers playing on pride and passion. Instead, they were layabouts more interested in enjoying the high-life at the five-star Grand Hotel than progressing in the World Cup.

One London newspaper said the Welsh team had been voted the best-looking of the 16 and that the players "are daily besieged by the beautiful blonde damsels of Sweden". Some of the players had been sent cuttings from relatives back home. The reports accused them of doing nothing but signing autographs and admiring the Swedish girls. Was this why Wales had played so poorly against the Mexicans? The allegations brought an angry response from captain Dave Bowen. "Anybody would think we were international playboys instead of an international football team out here to do a serious job of work," he said. "Ever since we met up at London two weeks ago the manager has trained us like slaves. I would be surprised if any of our boys sweat it out with their clubs more than they do with the Welsh team these days."

Bowen accused the media, who had also been harassing Billy Wright, the England captain, in Gothenburg over his relationship with one of the Beverley Sisters, of jumping to conclusions. The Grand Hotel might well be one of the best hotels in Sweden and a personal favourite of King Gustav. It might be a playground for the rich, situated on the tempting shores of the Baltic. Nevertheless, despite the surrounds, the Welsh squad were completely focused on the World Cup. "Many of us are married men with families," continued Bowen. "You can take it from me the boys are steaming mad to think that tripe like this can get into the Press."

There was another reason why the Welsh camp were tense, one which had nothing to do with the ethics of British journalism. There were rumblings that FIFA wanted to change the World Cup rules regarding the situation when two teams tied for second place in their group. Before the competition started, it was agreed in the event of two teams sharing second place that a play-off match would be held, to decide who joined the group leaders in the last eight. But now, before the third first-round games kicked-off, FIFA wanted goal difference to apply, thus dispensing with the need for play-offs. It said play-offs would congest the timetable and add strain on teams already playing matches every three days.

This news was worrying for Murphy. Wales were struggling to score goals and with Sweden still to come there was little hope of Wales improving their goal average. He was plotting a 0–0 against the Swedes to ensure his side finished on three points and secured a play-off with either Hungary or Mexico. If FIFA changed their minds then Murphy would have to rethink his strategy and play a more open, but more risky, game against the rampant hosts.

The Swedish FA, much to Murphy's delight, opposed the FIFA proposal, rightly claiming it contradicted FIFA's own directive, Article 22, paragraph six. However, the organisers had an ulterior motive. So far the World Cup had not made money. In fact, after the first two games, it was £130,000 in the red. The low attendances were blamed on poor weather and the live TV coverage. Only Group Four, involving Brazil and England, appeared to be filling the stadiums. Even matches involving Sweden were not sell-outs. The Rasunda Stadium had a capacity of more than 52,000 yet Sweden-Mexico attracted 34,000 and Sweden-Hungary attracted 39,000. Only 30,000 would turn up to watch Sweden-Wales. At 10pm on June 12, FIFA backed down. There would be play-offs if they were needed. As events turned out, it was a decision which kept Wales in the competition.

Murphy and the selectors were expected to make changes following the dire showing against Mexico. Webster, who played in the first two matches, was out. So too was Baker, who had replaced the injured Sullivan but struggled with the pace of the Mexico game. Out also was the injured Medwin who was suffering with a swollen ankle. Sullivan, who had recovered from his knee injury, was back at right-half while the new faces were Ron Hewitt, at inside-right, and Roy Vernon, at outside-right. As for John Charles, he was told to play almost in midfield. So, it was clear what Murphy's plan was – to hold out for a goalless draw.

"Jimmy Murphy knew I was hard-working and he wanted someone who would win the 50–50 balls," explains Hewitt. "If you were
an inside-forward you had to work hard. You had to feed the wingers. Murphy knew I could do the job."

Webster says, "I wasn't surprised to be dropped. Murphy wanted
a more defensive player. I thought I did OK in the two games that I
played in. As far as I was concerned I didn't think I was going to play
at all, so I thought I did well to play in two matches."

The team which Murphy picked to face Sweden was: Kelsey,
Williams, Hopkins, Sullivan, Mel Charles, Bowen, Vernon, Hewitt,
John Charles, Allchurch, Jones.

Murphy's strategy was to have all 11 men behind the ball. He
wanted to avoid defeat. If Wales lost and either Hungary or Mexico
won, then the Welsh would be knocked out. A draw, and they would
be guaranteed a place in the play-off match two days later. But
securing a point against Sweden would not be easy. As host nation,
they were inevitably psyched-up. They were also potential World
Cup winners.

Sweden had talent at its disposal since the late 1940s. At the 1948
Olympic Games in London the Swedish team, spearheaded by the
Gre-No-Li forward line of Gunnar Gren, Gunnar Nordahl and Nils
Liedholm, won gold. All three signed for Milan in 1949 and in the
1950/51 season they inspired the Milanese to win the Serie A title.
Nordahl and Liedholm won a second championship with Milan in
1955, although by then Gren – known as 'the Professor' – had moved
to Roma.

By the 1958 World Cup the Gre-No-Li combination was nearing
its end. Gren was now 38 and had returned to Gothenburg.
Liedholm was 36 but still with Milan where he had just enjoyed another splendid season. Nordahl had retired in 1957 at the age of 36.
In his six years with Milan, he scored an astonishing 210 goals in 257
appearances, still a Serie A record.

Gren, Nordahl and Liedholm were the first wave of super Swedes.
During the Fifties more exciting players emerged – left-winger
Lennart 'Nacka' Skoglund, right-winger Kurt Hamrin and centre-
half Julli Gustavsson. All three had followed the Gre-No-Li trio to
Italy, Skoglund with Inter, Hamrin with Padova (although he would
join Fiorentina after the World Cup) and Gustavsson with Atalanta.

But for years Sweden, because of its amateur ruling, failed to field
its best side. When Liedholm and friends went to seek fame and fortune in Italy they became professionals and were no longer eligible
for the national team. Still, in the 1950 World Cup the Swedes performed admirably without the Gre-No-Li combination, eventually

finishing third behind Uruguay and Brazil. However, the Swedish FA lifted the ban on professional players shortly before the 1958 tournament so at last the exiles could wear the yellow shirt of Sweden.

George Raynor was another reason for their emergence. The straight-talking Yorkshireman had an undistinguished career as a player, appearing for Aldershot and Rotherham, but it was a different story as far as management was concerned. On the recommendation of Stanley Rous, Raynor took control of Sweden in time for the 1950 competition in Brazil where they exceeded all expectations. After that, he tried his luck in Italy, with Lazio, but had a unsuccessful time and returned to Sweden.

A respected tactician who enjoyed coaching individuals Raynor, like Murphy, was hugely popular among the Swedish players. But unlike Murphy he was also one of the most thoroughly prepared managers in the World Cup. Immediately after Sweden had beaten Mexico in the opening match he dashed to his car and made the long trip to Sandviken to watch Wales play Hungary. "I had to persuade the police to let me tuck my car in behind the King's so I could escape quickly from the stadium," smiled Raynor. He insisted on travelling to watch potential opponents, studying their strengths and weaknesses. Twice he flew to Gothenburg after Sweden's afternoon matches to watch the host's likely quarter-final opponents, and in April, nearly two months before the competition began, he was in Cardiff watching the Wales-Northern Ireland match.

Wales had been given a pre-match boost before the all-important clash in the Rasunda Stadium. They would be facing a weakened Swedish side. The hosts, already safely into the last eight, had decided to rest five of their key players so they would be fresh for the knock-out stages. The five absentees were Liedholm, Mellberg, Simonsson, who scored two goals against Mexico, Gren and finally Hamrin, whose double strike had sunk Hungary three days earlier. The absence of Liedholm and particularly the lethal Hamrin was roundly cheered by the Welsh, but they would still have to be on their guard since Skoglund had not been dropped.

As expected, the Hungarians did not take this news so well. They needed to beat Mexico to stay in the World Cup but a Welsh victory, now a possibility since Raynor was without five of his best players, would render a win useless. They were about to lodge an official protest to FIFA but, realising they would do exactly the same thing as Sweden if they were in the same position, decided to let the matter rest. All the Hungarians could do was wait and hope. Their match against Mexico in Sandviken kicked-off at 7pm, more than three hours after the Sweden-Wales match in Stockholm had finished. Baroti was praying for a third successive win for the host nation.

For the second time in three days Wales marched onto the Rasunda Stadium's lush but heavy turf. They were intent on earning a draw, the draw that would secure their place in a play-off. Murphy told the players in the dressing room what Herbert Chapman had preached at Arsenal – "If our opponents don't score they can't beat us." He told his defenders to funnel back at the first sign of danger. The full-backs, Hopkins and Williams, were told to stick near centre-half Mel Charles. The wing-halves, Bowen and Sullivan, were warned not to be too adventurous while the wingers, Vernon and Jones, were ordered to pressurise the Swedes and help their defence. To cap it all, John Charles was asked to drop into a centre-half position alongside his brother, Mel, after the first 15 minutes when Wales planned to grab an early goal.

What followed was arguably the drabbest game of the 1958 series. But it was hardly unexpected. A team playing for a 0–0 result against a team which, on this day, was not really interested in winning.

"We took the field determined to get a draw," recalls Cliff Jones. The former Tottenham star says that as the two teams ran onto the field Skoglund told Mel Charles, 'It will be a draw today'. The Sweden match is one Jones prefers to forget, even though Wales held on for the point Murphy so desperately craved. Jones had a torrid 90 minutes and was well policed by the Swedish full-back Orvar Bergmark. "I had a nightmare. I had just done my national service and I felt lethargic about the game," recalls Jones. "I had played so much football that I'd lost my appetite for kicking a ball. Nothing went right for me and I was playing badly.

"Jimmy wasn't happy with me. He made one or two remarks at me. I remember him shouting, 'The ball is round Cliff! Let it roll!' But I was stale, mentally and physically. I'd played a lot of sport in the army – football, rugby, hockey, cricket – and I needed a rest, not a World Cup tournament."

Jones, to his credit, is quick to praise Bergmark. "I was stale but Bergmark played really well. He was a class player – very strong and very quick. He also had a good build for a defender. He was quite wiry. He was probably the best I've come up against. He knew what I wanted to do – push the ball and go, and he was ready for that. What I should have done was pass more. I was very predictable. I played right into his hands, but at least I gave 100 per cent."

It was Jones who missed Wales's best chance of the game early in the first-half. With just Swedish goalkeeper Svensson to beat from a few yards, the winger put his shot high over the bar. By that time

Sweden should have been two goals up but Skoglund, who like Jones had a poor 90 minutes, saw two of his efforts cleared off the line.

In the 12th minute John Charles, in one of his few threatening moments, glanced a header just inches wide of Svensson's post. Charles was hurt in that attack. As he went for the ball he clashed heads with a Swedish defender and suffered a cut left eyebrow as a result. The Juventus star was forced to play the second-half with a plaster above his left eye.

"We were up against it that day," says Charles whose defensive performance against Sweden was criticised by the Press. "They were the home side and we were trying to stay in the competition. Jimmy was really worked-up about this one. In the days leading up to that match Jimmy would go round the hotel dining-room when we were eating, saying, 'Don't forget! We've got to win this match! We'll go through!' We were a together team and we believed we could do it."

According to Charles, the fact that Sweden had dropped their star men for this match made little difference. "It wasn't the boost for us everyone thought. Players who come in to teams generally do better because they want to stay in the team, so the five new Swedish lads wanted to play well so they would be picked for the quarter-final."

Charles was not looking forward to this game. The defender who would be watching him was Gustavsson, who played for Atalanta. Charles knew Gustavsson well, they had played against each other in the 1957/58 season. In the two matches between Juventus and Atalanta, the Swede had marked the Welshman out of both games and had the honour of being the only Serie A defender to have had the better of Charles.

"Gustavsson was a very, very good player," remembers Charles. "He was good in the air and he was a good tackler. We had some good battles against each other. Sometimes he'd get the better of me, sometimes I'd get the better of him. We became good friends, in fact. One of my best friends at Juventus, Umberto Colombo, joined Atalanta and I used to go to Bergamo (the town in Lombardy where Atalanta are based) to see him. When I was there I got to know Gustavsson very well and we all used to go out to eat together." As it transpired Gustavsson saw little of Charles in this first-round clash since the Wales forward was playing as an extra defender.

Five minutes before half-time the Swedes had another chance to take the lead but again squandered it. This time the culprit was not Skoglund but Gosta Löfgren, one of the five new faces. He shot straight at Kelsey from just six yards out. At the interval the score was 0–0 and things were looking bright for Murphy. Sweden had far more of the play but without Liedholm, Hamrin and Simonsson they lacked the cutting edge they showed against Mexico and Hungary. Murphy's rearguard, especially Kelsey in goal, was looking unbreakable.

For the second-half, Wales continued with a defensive formation with John Charles lining-up alongside brother Mel in the heart of defence. For the first 10 minutes Murphy's players pressured the Swedish goal but then the match degenerated into the unambitious affair it had been in the first 45 minutes. Jones showed no signs of improvement, Charles was nowhere to be seen in attack while Vernon and Hewitt, on this day the latter was the best of the Welsh forwards, were more concerned in stopping Swedish attacks than supporting the isolated Allchurch.

The clock ticked on and, as far as Murphy was concerned, it looked like the match was petering out nicely into a goal-less draw. Masses of red shirts were camped protectively in front of Kelsey, waiting for Belgian referee Lucien Van Nuffel to blow the final whistle. Then, with just 15 minutes to go, it looked as if Wales were on their way home. Following a raid on Kelsey's goal the ball fell invitingly to Skoglund who was just two yards out and with an empty net in front of him. It looked a certain goal but amazingly Skoglund smashed his shot against the underneath of the crossbar. The ball rebounded onto Williams's knee before being cleared to safety. The Swedish players claimed the ball had crossed the line before it hit the West Bromwich Albion defender but Van Nuffel waved away their protests.

"The ball definitely did not cross the line," Kelsey said afterwards. "We were very lucky though because it was odds-on a Swedish goal."

Hopkins recalls, "We all thought he was going to score. It was more or less an open goal. I thought, 'Bloody hell, this is it!' But he missed. I couldn't believe he missed. I think he mis-kicked the ball or hit it too lazily. He should have scored really. It was a bad miss."

Skoglund, with his film star looks and unmistakable mop of blonde hair, was, at the time, the pin-up boy of Swedish football. But as he walked off the Rasunda pitch that evening on June 15 he was booed by his own supporters for fluffing four easy chances in the second-half, especially that one in the last quarter-of-an-hour. Skoglund died in 1975, at the age of 45. "He was a good player," recalls Charles who played against him so many times in Italy. "He had a great left-foot but he was a playboy and a bit of a boozer."

In the end Murphy's defensive tactics worked. The match finished 0–0. Svensson, in the Swedish goal, did not have to make a serious save from any of the Welsh players although his opposing number, Kelsey, was kept busy. The Arsenal man, whose secret tip was to rub chewing gum into his hands to improve his handling, had played the match of his life against the Swedes, thwarting attack after attack. By the end of the competition Kelsey would emerge as one of its best goalkeepers. Only Northern Ireland's Harry Gregg and Brazil's Gilmar could claim to have played as well as Kelsey.

"They definitely didn't play to win that day," adds Hopkins. "We thought they were going to come at us but they didn't and that helped us. It was the most boring game of the tournament. It was certainly boring for us."

Hopkins's defensive partner, Stuart Williams, says, "It was a good time to meet the Swedes. I marked Skoglund. He was a very tricky player. He was one of the star players and he knew it. He tried to take the mickey out of me. He was good on his left foot so I tried to get him on his right and stop him reaching the by-line. I handled him well."

Wales would be one of the teams which featured in the play-off, again in the Rasunda Stadium, in two days time. They returned to the Grand Hotel to await the result of the Hungary-Mexico game later that evening, a game which would decide who they faced in the play-off. If Murphy was expecting praise for masterminding a goal-less draw against Raynor's side, he was sadly mistaken. Afterwards, he was condemned for his team's approach. Dewi Lewis, writing in the *Western Mail*, said watching this match was like being "at a Sunday afternoon tea party" so unadventurous and non-aggressive were both teams.

The worst criticism came from the Swedish Press who were disillusioned with the form of John Charles. "What are Wales doing to John Charles?" cried *Aftonbladet*. The *Dagens Nyheter* newspaper went as far as to say, "He (Charles) was expected to be the personality of the World Cup. So far he is the flop." The newspaper claimed Charles was reluctant to take any risks for fear of being injured, thus incurring the wrath of his employers, Juventus.

"The Press always have a go," says Charles. "Jimmy wanted me to play a bit behind in that game. He put Ivor Allchurch in front of me and asked me to play like Di Stefano, although I could never play like Di Stefano. The type of game we played was part of our tactical plan. If we stopped Sweden scoring then we'd have a chance of staying in the World Cup. We were playing on the break all the time. I think Jimmy did the right thing. We couldn't score a lot of goals so he concentrated on defence. It was a dour game and it must have been terrible to watch. I felt sorry for the people who paid to see it. But

Jimmy was over the moon with the point. Back at the hotel he bought us all a drink which was rare."

Charles also remembers the curious behaviour of the Swedish fans. The forward, who played in Britain and Italy, was used to passion and emotion flowing from the terraces for the full 90 minutes. The Swedes, he says, were different. "They would be really quiet for a while, then all of a sudden they would start waving their flags and chanting," he recalls. "Then they went quiet, then it would start up all over again." What Charles almost certainly heard was Sweden's 1958 World Cup cry, 'Heia grabbar friskt humor, det or det som susen gor. Heia! Heia! Heia!' which translated means, 'Forward with good humour, that is what gives us the victory. Forward! Forward! Forward!' It was infrequently chanted during the host nation's World Cup games.

Murphy found himself on the defensive as soon as the match finished. The 29,800 crowd jeered the Welsh off the pitch while Murphy was held responsible for the most negative game of the 1958 World Cup. "Defence was our only way of getting a point. I think a draw was a fair result. From the Welsh angle we are well satisfied," said the defiant manager. "Taking our first three games as a whole I am very pleased. We are a very small country with few players to call upon. Whatever happens later in the tournament I think we've done well. When we left home nobody gave us a dog's chance. Yet we are unbeaten in three matches."

The hosts, like Wales, were happy with a point. They now topped Group Three with five points and it was impossible for either Hungary or Mexico to overtake them. Their prize was avoiding Brazil in Gothenburg. "Our drawn game with Wales helps us to convince people that we had no intention of throwing the match so as to keep Hungary out of the quarter-finals," said Erich Persson, the chairman of the Swedish selectors. He was responding to the Swedish Press who, before the Wales match, warned Raynor and his players they had a moral duty to try and win the game.

"Sweden underestimated us just like the Hungarians did," explains Hewitt, who made his first World Cup appearance against the Swedes. "When the referee blew at the end you could hear a pin drop. They thought they were going to hammer us. People were saying we were going to lose 6–0. We didn't notice the crowd but then again the crowd is quiet when things aren't going their way, and that day nothing went Sweden's way.

"In the dressing-room before the kick-off Murphy told us, 'They are no better than you! You are expected to lose, go out and show them you are here for something!' When we went onto the pitch we all felt six feet tall. A lot of teams would have been beaten before the kick-off, but not us and that was down to Murphy."

Hewitt, like Charles, defends the manager's tactics that day. "He didn't want us to leave any gaps and I agree with what he did. He did the right thing. I think if we tried to beat Sweden we would have lost."

The draw put the Welsh selectors in an embarrassing position. They were sure Sweden were going to win the game, so sure they had booked their flight back to London after this match. They did not count on their country progressing to the next round or, at the very least, earning a play-off. "Do you know what they did? They had to fly back to London, book their tickets and come back over again," recalls Mel Charles. "What can you say? It was unbelievable." John Charles adds, "I remember the day they were leaving. They were in the hotel foyer waiting for transport to the airport. They were crying their eyes out. 'Goodbye and all the best' they told us. They weren't sure they would be able to come back. It depended if there were seats available when they got back to London. It was an unbelievable sight." The selectors were able to return to Stockholm the following day.

Ken Jones is criticial of their decision to book their flight after the third match. "It's typical of the way Wales do things. You have to admit, England do things tidy but with Wales it's an absolute shambles. Most of the selectors couldn't see from the stands to the pitch so how they picked the team anyway I don't know. Still, we had a great day without them in the hotel. We could walk around with a glass of beer in our hands without having to worry who was around." This staggering lack of faith did nothing to endear them to the players, most of whom already felt detached from the selectors. "The only one who had faith in us," says Webster, "was Jimmy Murphy."

By 9pm that night the Welsh knew who their play-off opponents were. It was Hungary. In the Jernvallen the Magyars easily disposed of Mexico 4–0. Tichy, not Sándor, was proving to be Hungary's most potent weapon and he put Baroti's side 1–0 up in the first-half. A minute after the break Tichy bagged his second of the evening and his third of the competition. That was the end of the Mexican challenge. Sándor made it 3–0 after 54 minutes and, to complete a miserable night for Mexico, poor Juan González scored an own-goal on the hour. After 11 World Cup matches Mexico had still to register a win. In the three tournaments he played, Carbajal, their goalkeeper, conceded 21 goals.

Wales were joined in the play-offs by Northern Ireland, another of the nations written off before the tournament started. They performed brilliantly against the West Germans in Malmö. Doherty's men were just 10 minutes from glory when Seeler pounced to make it 2–2. McParland put the Irish in front after 17 minutes but Rahn, to the delight off the 10,000 German supporters in the 22,000 crowd, levelled three minutes later. However, McParland hit his second of the match after nearly an hour to put Northern Ireland back in the lead. With Gregg, who had twisted his ankle and had to ask his defenders to take the goal-kicks, saving everything in sight and McParland running the German defence ragged, it looked like the Irish would pull off the biggest upset of the 1958 series. Then, Seeler, who had been foiled by Gregg throughout the game, unleashed an unstoppable 25–yard shot past the despairing Manchester United goalkeeper.

Victory was snatched at the death but the Irish were still in the tournament which was more than could be said for Argentina. The fancied South Americans, who many tipped to win the Jules Rimet Trophy, crashed 6–1 to Czechoslovakia in Halsingborg. The match was effectively over at half-time when the Czechs, who had to win to earn a play-off, were 3–0 up thanks to goals from Dvorak and two from Zikan. It got worse for the Argentinians in the second-half even though Corbatta pulled one back in the 65th minute with his second penalty of the tournament. Jiri Feureisl made it 4–1 with 20 minutes remaining, then Vaclav Hovorka scored two further goals to make it six. This result remains Argentina's heaviest defeat in the World Cup. For the Czechs, it meant a showdown with the Irish. As for Argentina, the result prompted angry scenes when the team returned to Buenos Aires. As they left the airport the players were greeted with rotten tomatoes and stones. The headquarters of the Argentinian FA was also attacked.

In Group Two the Scots were finally put out of their misery. Their 2–1 defeat at the hands of France in Örebro meant they were the first of the British sides to return home. France raced into a 2–0 lead. Predictably, the goals came from Kopa and Fontaine. For the latter, it was his sixth goal in three games, although John Hewie missed a penalty shortly after Kopa's opening goal. Sammy Baird made it 2–1 with 25 minutes remaining but only heroics from goakeeper Bill Brown, making his debut for Scotland, stopped the French adding to their tally. For the Scots, so disappointing in Switzerland four years earlier, it was another dismal World Cup showing.

In Group Four, England joined Wales and Northern Ireland in the play-offs, but only after being given a fright by the Austrians in Boras. Needing a win to join Brazil in the last eight, England fell behind after 15 minutes when Koller beat McDonald from 25 yards. At the break, Austria led 1–0 and a group of English sailors in the stadium, sensing a black day for English football, played *The Last Post*.

This was expected to be a relatively easy match for Winterbottom's side. They had recovered well against the Russians and had matched Brazil in their last match. As for Austria, they had lost both games, conceding five and scoring none. Haynes made it 1–1 after 60 minutes and the 16,800 crowd sensed an England winner in the last half-an-hour. But it was Austria who scored a second, through Alfred Körner whose shot went in off the post. It looked all over for England, who once more refused to select Bobby Charlton, but 12 minutes from the end Kevan equalised with a ferocious shot.

Bobby Robson, who had a goal disallowed against the Russians, had another ruled out in this match. The linesman, Istvan Zsolt, claimed Robson had handled the ball before firing it past Rudolf Szanwald. Had it been given, England would have made the quarter-finals. Now they would have to face the Soviet Union for the third time in a month.

In Gothenburg the Brazilians made sure off topping the group with a 2–0 win over the Russians who had recalled Netto, now fully fit, into the side. A crowd of 51,000, the biggest of the first-round, saw Vavà score both goals, the first after three minutes and the second after 77 minutes. Brazil's manager, Feola, chose Zito, Garrincha and Pelé for the first time in the 1958 World Cup. After he scored his second, the tall Vavà, an untypical Brazilian striker, was mobbed by his team-mates who piled on top of him as if they were in a rugby scrum. As a result, Vavà was carried off the pitch injured and needed five minutes to recover before he rejoined the action.

Safely through to the next stage were West Germany, France, Yugoslavia, Sweden and Brazil. The teams forced into a play-off were Northern Ireland and Czechoslovakia from Group One, Wales and Hungary from Group Three and England and the Soviet Union from Group Four. The casualties after three matches were Argentina, Scotland, Mexico and Austria.

CHAPTER TEN

GLORY IN STOCKHOLM

THE play-offs were scheduled for June 17, just two days after the last first-round matches. For the second time in nine days Wales would meet Hungary to decide who had the unenviable honour of facing Brazil, the Group Four champions and World Cup favourites, in the quarter-final in Gothenburg.

Both sides were confident of victory. Wales felt they should have beaten the Hungarians in the first match at Sandviken while Hungary had just put four past Mexico and were widely tipped to beat the Welsh in the Rasunda Stadium. Murphy, however, was adamant his team would reach the next round. "People have forgotten our feat in holding Hungary to a draw," said Murphy the day before the play-off. " We almost beat Hungary in that match. We will beat them tomorrow. Those people who say we can't attack can expect a shock."

He made just one change to the team that drew with Sweden. Vernon made way for Medwin, who was now fit. Hewitt, who had done well against the hosts, kept his place at inside-right ahead of Webster. John Charles, who suffered a head wound against the Swedes, had four stitches in his left eyebrow but was fit enough to play. More significantly, Murphy released him from his defensive duties and asked him to play as a true centre-forward.

The team which faced Hungary was: Kelsey, Williams, Hopkins, Sullivan, Mel Charles, Bowen, Medwin, Hewitt, John Charles, Allchurch, Jones. The only difference between this line-up and the one that faced Hungary in Sandviken was Hewitt for Webster.

Wales's skipper, Dave Bowen, shared Murphy's pre-match confidence. "Wales always do better when we are the underdog. They told us we would beat Mexico 6–0. They said we would murder Sweden. This time all the bets will be against us. Hungary are a powerful side. They will bring out the best in us." Bowen was right, Wales were the underdogs. After the opening match, their performances had deteriorated. First there was the dismal 90 minutes against Mexico, then came the Sweden match where the Welsh hardly made an attempt on Svensson's goal.

Wales could count themselves lucky they were still in the competition. Had FIFA had their way, Wales, following results in the last first-round matches, would have been joining Argentina, Scotland, Mexico and Austria on the next flight home because Hungary, after their 4–0 win over Mexico, had a superior goal average. However, Hungary's goal average would count if, after extra-time, the teams were both drawn. To reach the next round Wales had to win, something they had yet to do in Sweden.

The Hungarian team was more or less unchanged from the one that played in Sandviken although Hidegkuti, so anonymous against the Welsh more than a week ago, had not played since that opening game. Baroti, it appeared, had finally won his argument with the head of selectors, Barcs. The great Hungarian would eventually retire from football after the World Cup. Dropped also was Sándor who had not lived up to his reputation in Sweden.

Bozsik, who scored Hungary's goal in the earlier 1–1 draw, now played in Hidegkuti's position while right-winger Laszlo Budai, who played his first match against the Mexicans, replaced Sándor. Wales also had to watch out for Tichy. Before the competition he was tipped as Hungary's secret weapon and with three goals in three games he had lived up to expectations.

In Sandviken, Hungary won all the pre-match battles, but in Stockholm it was Wales's turn. This time it was the Welsh who wore the red shirts. This time it was the Hungarians who had to make the 125-mile trek to the stadium. And this time it was Bowen who won the toss. In fact, it was the first time in the competition that Bowen had won. Grosics, and not Kelsey, would start facing the strong evening sun that lit up the Rasunda Stadium.

Wales started with these psychological advantages but Murphy was still unhappy with the choice of referee, Russian Nikolai Latychev – an Iron Curtain referee in charge of a match involving an Iron Curtain team. Murphy feared Latychev would favour the Hungarians. As the match unfolded the Welshman's fears were realised.

The 52,400 capacity Rasunda Stadium was practically deserted for this Group Three play-off. A crowd of only 2,832, by far and away the smallest of the 1958 World Cup, turned up, perhaps scared Wales would defend en masse just as they did against the Swedes. The atmosphere was more akin to a pre-season friendly than a vital World Cup game, with the Rasunda's vast expanses of concrete exposed by the pitiful attendance. "It was dead inside the stadium," says Hewitt. "I can remember looking around when the anthems were being played. I couldn't believe how empty it was." Medwin, too, was stunned by the low turnout. "There were only 2,000 people and most of those tickets were complimentary. It was sad so few people were there because it turned out to be a great game, one of the best of the tournament."

Before the kick-off the Hungarian players appeared uncomfortable and tense. News from home had not been good. The previous day Imre Nagy, the leader of the Hungarian Uprising, had been executed by his country's communist regime. The handful of Hungarian supporters in the Rasunda crowd, situated behind both goals, hemmed their flags with black in protest at their government's brutality. They also chanted Free Hungary songs. The players saw these flags, they also heard the songs. Officials inside the stadium, keen to keep politics and football apart, asked the Hungarians to remove the banners. Some obeyed, most did not. Those who did not were thrown out of the stadium at half-time.

Wales started the stronger of the two sides. Grosics saved brilliantly from a John Charles header but then Latychev began to show signs of Iron Curtain bias, denying the Welsh two clear penalties, both involving Charles. First, as he went for a loose ball in the area he was hauled down at the waist by Antal Kotász but Latychev ignored Wales's protests. Then, a minute later, Charles was shoved in the back by Mátrai, Hungary's gangly full-back who, in the first match in Sandviken, had tripped Allchurch inside the penalty area when the Welsh forward looked certain to score the winner.

"Murphy built us up before the game," recalls John Charles. "He shouted at us, 'We can beat this lot!' He told us they were no better than us, that they hadn't got Puskas anymore, that they were an ordinary side living on a reputation. We left our dressing room thinking we could beat them."

After 33 minutes, and against the run of play, Hungary, just as they did in Sandviken, snatched the lead. Tichy, who had scored a stunning goal against Sweden, repeated the feat against Kelsey. With most of the Welsh team in the Hungarian half probing for the first goal Budai sprinted towards Kelsey and squared the ball to Tichy. Williams perhaps should have intercepted and the Hungarian forward, standing on the corner of Kelsey's six-yard box, fired a low, unstoppable shot inside the near post and past the Arsenal goalkeeper. It was his fourth goal in as many games.

Wales now had to score twice to make the quarter-finals. At half-time they trailed 1–0 but they still had 45 minutes left and they were playing their best football of the World Cup. Jones, indifferent in the first three matches, was giving the Hungarian defenders a headache on the left-wing. Allchurch was oozing class at inside-forward and Charles, despite being hacked down at every turn, was showing just why Juventus valued his legs at £150,000.

Latychev, shortly after the interval, denied Wales yet another penalty. Again the victim was Charles. He tried to reach a Medwin corner but Sipos, right in front of the referee who was standing on the 18–yard line, held the forward down by his hips. For the third time the Russian official waved play on.

Wales were beginning to dominate and the equaliser was not far away. It came 10 minutes after the break and was one of the most breathtaking goals of the World Cup. Bowen took a throw-in. He found John Charles who had, only seconds earlier, limped back onto the field after being scythed down yet again by Kotász. Charles lobbed a forward ball to Allchurch who was unmarked but still 25 yards from Grosics's goal. Allchurch, with his left foot, curled the ball past the outstretched Hungarian into the left-hand corner.

"It was an amazing goal but Ivor was that sort of player," says Charles. "He could hit a ball from anywhere, with his left or right foot. I remember looking at the Welsh bench after the goal. Jimmy was jumping up and down on the touchline."

Hewitt adds, "We couldn't catch Ivor after he scored. The Hungarians had been so busy with John they had left room for other forwards like Ivor. It was a fantastic goal and you don't forget goals like that. It couldn't have happened to a nicer chap. Ivor was both a gentleman and a gentle man." Kelsey, too, described Allchurch's goal as the one of the finest he had ever seen.

Ken Leek was sitting on the bench with Murphy and the rest of the squad when Allchurch hit Wales's third goal of World Cup '58. "I was sitting next to Ken Jones. At first we didn't think it had gone in. Then we saw the 'keeper picking the ball from inside the net. We went absolutely crazy. It was a terrific goal, and a typical Ivor goal as well." Cliff Jones agrees. "When you think about it, all of Ivor's goals were great because they were never scored inside the penalty area."

Wales were back in the hunt, but 1–1 would not be enough. If there was no change after extra-time the Hungarians would progress thanks to their better goal average. They needed another goal. If the play-off was to see a third goal, it would surely be scored by the resur-gent Welsh, not the demoralised Magyars. "As soon as we equalised the Hungarians started panicking. They thought they were going to win this match, but after Ivor's equaliser we were on top and they knew it," recalls Medwin.

Interestingly, Hopkins sensed discord among the Hungarian

players. "They were having a go at each other throughout the game. We didn't know what they were saying because we couldn't understand them but you could tell they were having a niggle. They were pointing and shouting at each other. I could tell there was something not right in the team." Had the bleak reports from Budapest triggered their unease?

Hungary's tackling before Allchurch's goal was crude. After, it was positively x-rated. They sensed the match was slipping away from them and resorted to hacking down every Welsh player in sight, particularly John Charles. "They kicked hell out of me and the referee didn't give me any protection," remembers Charles, whose Gentle Giant reputation was really put to the test that summer evening. "They were losing their rag, especially after we scored. They started on me after five minutes. One of the defenders got hold of my shirt and pulled me down. They were kicking Ivor as well, then one of them charged into Cliff. That was then the trouble started. Derrick (Sullivan) got involved and started kicking their players back. That's what happens in football.

"In the first match, the Hungarians shoved and held. This time they were fouling with their feet. It was unbelievable. In all the games I played, in Italy, in England and for Wales, this was the worst." His brother Mel, from his centre-half position, watched the Hungarians cut down his team-mates. "It got dodgy after Ivor scored. They started playing the man, not the ball. John, Ivor and Cliffie were getting it. They were kicking Cliffie up in the air. We were on top and they were getting very robust, kicking out all the time. I was lucky because I was facing them so I could see what they were up to. I would hit them back whenever I could.

"This was without doubt the roughest game I've ever played in. They decided they had to get John. They were getting him with their elbows and going in over the top. John was placid, he would take it like a gentleman. But I was different to John. If they hit me, I hit them back. I'd hit them with my shoulder. In a 50–50 situation I'd just put all my weight behind it."

Each time John Charles was knocked down he would get up, dust himself down and walk away, sometimes even with a grin on his face. But there was one foul Charles remembers to this day. It came with about 20 minutes remaining. It was the foul which would lead to quarter-final heartbreak. "The ball came to me and I chested it down. Then someone whacked me on the back of my right leg, the one I kicked with." The guilty Hungarian was the mean-looking centre-half, Sipos, who had committed foul after foul on the Juventus forward eight days earlier. "That finished me. I couldn't really play after that." He did not know it at the time but Charles had suffered a strained buttock ligament, an injury which forced him to limp heavily for the remainder of the second-half. Wales, in effect, were down to 10 men since these were pre-substitute days. This made the performance, and the final result, even more startling.

Shortly after Allchurch's equaliser, Jones, playing his best game of the competition so far, looked set to score that precious second goal. An inch-perfect diagonal ball from Mel Charles, who was just inside the Hungarian half, beat Mátrai and fell to the Tottenham winger who controlled it on his chest and had just Grosics to beat. "I took it beautifully and waited for the ball to drop. I was around eight yards from goal. Then I hit it on the half-volley with my right foot. It went straight over the bar," sighs Jones, who had also spurned an easy chance against Sweden. "The expressions on the faces of the players summed up what they thought of that miss. Nobody said a word to me as I made my way back into our own half. It was a really bad miss."

Had Hungary scored a second goal or the result stayed at 1–1 then Jones may well have been vilified back home. However, a childhood friend spared his blushes with just 14 minutes left. Medwin, who went to the same school as Jones, St Helen's Primary School in Swansea, cheekily placed the ball beyond the diving Grosics following an horrendous mix-up involving the Hungarian goalkeeper and full-back Laszlo Sárosi. It was the goal that secured Wales's first, and only, victory in the World Cup. It was the goal that put Wales into the last eight.

Medwin, who described the goal as the most important of his career, recalls the moment he sent Hungary packing from the 1958 competition. "Grosics was taking a goal-kick and he passed to the full-back who was around six to eight yards away from him. The full-back wasn't expecting the pass and I nipped in before him and ran into the penalty area. John was also in the area, free and unmarked. The 'keeper thought I was going to pass to him and left a couple of yards space between him and the near post. He was looking at me but was moving ever so slightly towards John. As I ran towards the goal I wasn't sure what I was going to do, whether I was going to shoot or square it to John, but Grosics made up my mind for me. There was that little gap and I decided to shoot."

Medwin's shot was low, hard and accurate. Wales, with less than 15 minutes remaining, had one foot in Gothenburg. For Medwin, the goal was a personal triumph. Along with Kelsey, John Charles, Jones and Allchurch he was one of Murphy's elite players yet in the two first-round games, where he played at inside-right rather than on the wing, he had little joy. Then he missed the Sweden match through injury. For Medwin, the 1958 World Cup had been close to becoming an anti-climax, but now the Tottenham star had made his mark on the competition.

"Grosics had no chance with Ivor's shot but with me he made his mind up too early and he gave me the room I needed to put the ball between him and the post. That was his mistake," adds Medwin. "Grosics was right, I would have passed to John, but he shouldn't have moved over."

Wales, after dominating most of the second-half, were deservedly ahead. Murphy had promised a more attack-minded strategy and he delivered. "After Terry had scored I looked up into the stands and the Welsh selectors were dancing up and down," laughs Charles. "And Jimmy and Jack Jones were jumping and hugging each other. There were some unbelievable scenes."

Medwin's goal shattered Hungary who were still reeling from Allchurch's wonder-strike 26 minutes earlier. The players started rowing among themselves, some even had tears in their eyes. Murphy now changed tactics, reverting to the formation used against the Swedes. Charles was brought back into defence with Medwin, Jones, and Allchurch playing on the break.

As for Hungary, they were a team which had lost its discipline. With eight minutes left, Hewitt was penalised for charging Grosics. While Latychev was talking to Hewitt, the pint-sized Cardiff City player was pole-axed to the ground by Dezso Bundzsák. Incredibly, Latychev took no action against Hungary's inside-left.

Hewitt was a marked man. Four minutes later, he was on the receiving end of arguably the worst challenge of the competition. The culprit was, once again, the gigantic centre-half Sipos. "I was making a forward run. I didn't even have the ball," recalls Hewitt, "The next thing I knew I was on the floor and there was this pain in my left leg." Hewitt, just seconds earlier, had fooled Sipos. The Hungarian defender had taken umbrage and aimed a swipe at the Welsh inside-right, catching him on his left thigh. "I didn't see him do it but I saw him just walk away. He didn't give a bugger. Bastard."

The challenge incensed the Welsh bench. A furious Murphy sprinted onto the touchline to remonstrate with the linesman. "Jimmy went absolutely mad," recalls Leek. "He wasn't one for going onto the pitch but he did that day. There were some nasty tackles flying about and Jimmy got worked up because the referee and linesmen weren't doing anything about it." Ken Jones, too, displayed his anger but in a different way to Murphy. "The first time the ball rolled out of play after the kick on Hewitt," adds Leek, "Ken

picked up the ball and just booted it out of the ground!" For his display of petulance, the reserve goalkeeper was fined £25 by FIFA and
£25 by his club, Cardiff City. "The guy nearly kicked our man in
half," says an unrepentant Jones today. 'When I kicked the ball away
the ref came over to the bench and took my name."

It looked as if Latychev, who had already refused to award Wales
three blatant penalties, was again going to show leniency towards the
Hungarians by refusing to take action against Sipos. However, a full
four minutes after the foul had been committed, Latychev bowed to
common sense and ordered the burly defender off the field. To a cho-
rus of boos, Sipos slowly made his way to the dressing room.

That meant both teams were down to 10 men. For Hewitt too, the
match was over. He was later taken to a hospital in Stockholm and
diagnosed with a nerve injury which paralysed his leg. He would
recover in time for the quarter-final.

"Sipos deserved to go, no doubt about it," says Hewitt. "I don't
hold anything against him because he wanted to win. I probably
would have done the same. I wasn't there for the show, I wanted to
win. So did he. But the Hungarians were stupid. They let themselves
down. They ruined their reputation."

In the last four minutes the Hungarians made a final push for the
equaliser and in the dying seconds, the Magyars nearly snatched a
goal. Hungary were awarded a free-kick on the edge of the Welsh
penalty area. Bozsik chipped tantalisingly over the defensive wall.
Fenyvesi ghosted around the block of Welsh shirts and headed towards Kelsey's goal. The ball was heading for the far corner of the
net but Kelsey flung himself at the ball and managed to palm it round
the post for a corner.

"Jimmy was on the halfway line shouting at the ref to blow his
whistle," says John Charles. "He would have a little drink of whisky
during the match and I saw him drinking from his flask on the touchline, waiting for the end." The end was not far away. After the subse-
quent corner Latychev called time on the most exciting, and
dramatic, of the three 1958 World Cup play-off matches. The Hungarians sloped off the pitch, shamed and humiliated while the Welsh
players embraced each other in the centre-circle. "The selectors came
into the dressing room, dancing and jigging," adds the former
Juventus striker. "Jimmy was pretty quiet considering what had happened. He just said, 'Well done' to all the players, but in the hotel
later that night he started singing *Land of Hope and Glory*."

In 48 hours time Wales would face Brazil, favourites to lift the trophy, over in Gothenburg. "I am a proud man tonight," remarked
Murphy after the play-off. "I still think my policy of playing for a

draw against Sweden was the correct one for I knew the lads had it in them to beat these Hungarians, despite their robust tactics. Whatever happens on Thursday the players have done Wales proud."

Charles, whose body was covered bruises, said the players had always been confident of beating the 1954 runners-up. "I knew the boys would do it before I went on the field. There was that feeling in the camp – a determination which could not be dismissed."

Hopkins says, "When we made it 2–1 I knew we were going to win. They were in a right state and they couldn't get their game back on track. They started to get dirty when they were losing and they were doing a lot of ankle tapping. They thought they were going to go through easily, but they didn't play as well as they could have done. The 1958 World Cup was the biggest disappointment for Hungarian football in the last 40 years, because they were expected to win and they didn't."

The Hungarian players emerged from their dressing-room tired and silent. Their country was at a low ebb and in Sweden they had failed to give their people at home anything to cheer about. They were a team that had lost its majesty. Only Tichy and Bozsik could return to Budapest with their heads held high. Considering the toll the uprising had taken on the national team nobody expected Hungary to repeat their performances of 1954, but their violent tackling in Sweden meant nobody was sorry to see them go.

"We counted on a victory against Wales," said Baroti, "but our young players were not strong enough." The Magyars may have been disturbed by political unrest in Hungary but that could not take the shine off Wales's victory. In the match at Sandviken, many thought Murphy's men should have taken both points. Nine days later, in a near-deserted Rasunda Stadium, they finished the job. Of all the Hungarian players only Bozsik would speak to the media about the play-off defeat. To his credit he praised the victors. "The Welshmen played well, better than we had expected. They play hard but fair football and they have John Charles who is always dangerous."

Another of the British teams joined Wales in the quarter-finals that night – not England but Northern Ireland. The Irish pulled off another play-off surprise by beating Czechoslovakia 2–1 in Malmö. Despite winning the first match, Doherty's side were given no hope in the play-off with the Czechs who were quoted at 1–4 on to win. Those odds may have had something to do with Gregg, a casualty of the West Germany game, being unfit to play. He was replaced by Norman Uprichard who kept goal when Northern Ireland beat Italy 2–1 in January.

It looked as if the bookmakers' odds would be justified. After 19 minutes Zikan headed the Czechs in front following a mix-up between Uprichard and full-back Willie Cunningham who both failed to cut out a Czech free-kick. Just seconds before half-time the Irish equalised. McParland, who was having a terrific tournament, fired home after Dolejsi saved three times from Cush. After 90 minutes the score was still 1–1. Now it was extra-time and the Czechs were reduced to 10 men after right-half Titus Bubernik was sent off for spitting at French referee Maurice Guigue. The Irish were in no position to take advantage of their numerical superiority. Uprichard had broken a bone in his left hand and was in agony every time he touched the ball while defender Robert Peacock was limping. Peacock was ordered to play the rest of the match in attack where his task was to distract the Czech defenders.

The winner came after 99 minutes. McParland was again the hero. From a Blanchflower free-kick he volleyed past the bemused Dolejsi into the roof of the net. It was McParland's fifth goal of the World Cup and it booked Northern Ireland's place in the quarter-final against France in Norrköping.

England's campaign came to an end in Gothenburg. There, they unluckily lost 1–0 to the Soviet Union. The selectors, who had nine fresh players to choose from, changed the English right-wing for the play-off, dropping the Eddie Clamp-Bobby Robson-Brian Douglas combination for Ronnie Clayton at right-half, Peter Brabrook at outside-right and Peter Broadbent at inside-right.

The Russians dominated the first half-an-hour but then Brabrook missed the chance of a lifetime. With 37 minutes gone Broadbent drew out Yashin and squared to Brabrook who had the goal at his mercy, but he panicked and toe-poked the ball straight to the grateful Russian goalkeeper. England started the second-half aggressively. Kevan went close and Brabrook twice hit the post and had a goal disallowed for handball. But in the 63rd minute a careless goalkick from McDonald cost them the match. His feeble effort rolled straight to the surprised Iurii Fallin who passed to Simonian. It was two against one – Simonian and Anatolii Ilyin against Wright. Before Wright could make a tackle Simonian pushed the ball to the unmarked Ilyin. His low shot beat McDonald and went in off the post.

England, one of the favourites, were out. Their record in Sweden was three draws, one defeat. The Press, inevitably, were far from happy. England's dismal World Cup record continued. Winterbottom and the selectors flew home to face the music, especially over the refusal to play Bobby Charlton in any of the matches. For

England, it was a case of how different it might have been had Byrne, Edwards and Taylor been alive.

Two of the four British teams were through to the last eight. Not England and Scotland, as many would have expected, but Wales and Northern Ireland.

The night of the victorious play-off the Welsh selectors held a collar-and-tie party in the Copacabana Club, a smart nightclub built underneath the Grand Hotel. The post-match celebrations, however, were marred by an unsavoury incident involving Webster and one of the club's waiters, Verner Felt, which climaxed with Webster headbutting Felt. As Ken Jones recalls, "We didn't go straight to the club – 'the Big Five' went into Stockholm on the train first. We wanted to go to the party when the selectors, their wives and Jimmy Murphy were out of the way, otherwise it would've been 'What are you drinking?' and 'What are you up to?' If we got there at around midnight there was a good chance they'd have gone."

When 'the Big Five' arrived Murphy and the selectors had gone to bed. The rest of the players were still in the club. "We arrived at about 1.30am. We'd had a few drinks in Stockholm and we had beer stains all over our ties," says the former goalkeeper. "I remember Kenny Leek walking onto the stage, grabbing the microphone from the cabaret artist and singing songs. The bouncers let him sing one song. It was terrible, his speech was quite slurred. Then he wanted to sing *Hen Wlad Fy Nhadau*, but by then everyone had had enough and they pulled him off the stage." Then, a few minutes later, Jones noticed a skirmish. Webster was being thrown out of the club after headbutting one of the waiters.

According to the former Manchester United player, the aggravation was over a girl. "I think he thought I was eyeing up his girlfriend. I had been in the club a few times and there had been tension between me and this waiter. I was chatting with this girl. I think it must have been his girlfriend. Every time he walked past me he'd nudge me. He would eye-ball me as well. I didn't know it was his girlfriend. That night, as I walked past him, I thought he was going to grab me, so I butted him. I ended up knocking three of his teeth out."

Mel Charles, who was sitting at a table with his brother, Allchurch and Cliff Jones, recalls, "The waiter went flying. He ended up on John's lap and glasses went everywhere." Webster continues, "There were three bongo players in the club that night. They smuggled me into their room after what happened. They were going to Finland the next day and asked me if I wanted to go with them because of all the trouble I was in. I seriously thought about it."

Medwin remembers the scene in the Copacabana after the

headbutt. "John (Charles) grabbed Colin and lifted him a foot of the ground and carried him out. I remember Ken Jones looking up at John and saying, 'Now put him down John, or I'll land one on you!'" Jones admits confronting Charles as he tried to drag Webster out of the club. "I defended Colin. I had to – he was my mate. I got involved in a melee but I didn't do any damage. It was all down to over-exuberance. It had been a night of elation. We had done so well. The booze was in, the wit was out, but this one spark caused a fire."

The manager of the Copacabana Club threatened to call the police and there was talk of Felt bringing an assault charge against Webster. The Welsh FA, desperate to sweep the incident under the carpet, agreed to pay Felt compensation. John Charles, the self-styled ambassador for the squad, organised a collection and every player was asked to chip in £2 of their spending allowance.

"We sorted it out in the end," says Charles. "Colin apologised to the waiter and we had a whip-round. We paid him to keep quiet because if the papers got hold of it there would have been hell to pay. The waiter wasn't really in a bad way. He lost a couple of teeth but apart from that he was all right. Jimmy knew what had happened and he was going mad with Colin. He wanted to send him home but I said we should keep him in case there were any injuries (ironically, Webster would replace the injured Charles in the Brazil match). Herbert Powell was frightened to death about the whole thing being made public, because it would give Wales a bad name."

Following the whip-round Felt signed the following letter. "I hereby acknowledge the receipt of Kronor 300 (Three hundred kronor) as compensation for damage and injuries received on the premises of Grand Hotel Soltsjöbaden as a result of an assault on my person by Mr Colin Webster. Upon receipt of this sum I have no further claims. Stockholm 18th June 1958."

That same day a players' meeting was held in the room Ken Jones and Colin Baker shared. "The senior pros gave us a rap on the knuckles," says Jones. "John called me an arsehole. I don't know if Colin was dealt with privately. I thought I was on the next plane home and that my mum was going to kill me, but John had seen the manager of the club and agreed the team would pay for all the damage. The senior pros said we'd let the team and our country down. That's when it came home to roost. What we did was completely and utterly wrong and we were lucky to get away with it,"

Felt may have dropped any potential action but all 18 players were now banned from the club. The uneasy atmosphere inside the Grand Hotel would not last long – the Welsh squad were leaving Soltsjöbaden early the following morning for Gothenburg. "They didn't have to ban us," adds Jones. "We were too embarrassed to go back in there anyway. It wasn't just the players who were in the Copacabana at the time. There were men in dicky-bows and ladies in evening dresses. It was a nice club and all this happened in front of them."

The players had mixed feelings regarding the £2 they were each asked to pay. For some, like John Charles, Hewitt and Medwin, it was not such a big deal. "Lads are lads," explains Big John. "Footballers all stick together. I was embarrassed, but this is what some footballers get up to." Others, however, were not as forgiving. "Why should we have had to pay it?" says Mel Charles. " In those days £2 was a lot of money. If I remember correctly we had to pay the waiter £76. We gave £2 each. Even Jimmy Murphy paid up. Colin paid the rest, and deservedly so."

The selectors did manage to prevent the Copacabana Club fiasco leaking out. If it had, there is little doubt the Welsh would have become the villains of the 1958 series. Across Sweden the rest of the competing teams – notably Brazil, Northern Ireland and Mexico – had charmed the Swedes with their friendly, easy-going manner. (Because of the tremendous spirit displayed by teams on and off the pitch, the 1958 World Cup became known as "the friendly World Cup"). Wales, only hours after their famous victory, risked souring the competition.

"We were annoyed with Colin," says Hopkins. "It was a silly incident, stupid. It was a spur of the moment thing and we all apologised to the waiter. It was very embarrassing because we had made a lot of friends in Soltsjöbaden. It was a good job it was kept quiet. If the story got out it could have got nasty. We would have been branded the hooligans of the World Cup."

CHAPTER ELEVEN

BRAZIL

THE day after the play-off the Welsh party reluctantly waved good-bye to Soltsjöbaden and the Grand Hotel, their home for the last 16 days. The players had become attached to the picturesque town which, in turn, had adopted the Welsh team.

The locals always turned up to watch Murphy and his players at work on the local training ground and the players themselves were only too willing to sign autographs and pose for pictures.

The presence of a World Cup team had brought a great deal of excitement to this quiet and secluded resort. John Charles and company had become quite an attraction. "There were tears from the youngsters in the local café where we had swigged Coca-Cola and played records in the evenings," Kelsey recalled of their departure.

Their destination was Gothenburg on the west coast, the second-biggest city in Sweden, where mighty Brazil were waiting. Their limbs still aching from that gruelling clash with the uncompromising Hungarians, the Welsh players boarded the plane at Bromma Airport which would fly them to Gothenburg's Torslanda Airport. The Welsh base for the quarter-final was the Fars Hatt Hotel in Kungälv, a small town just outside Gothenburg which Kelsey described as dull compared to Soltsjöbaden.

Murphy, with just 24 hours to prepare for the Brazilian match, had plenty to worry about. He had yet to see Brazil play and he knew little of their methods. After arriving in Gothenburg the first thing Murphy did was to find English-speakers who had seen Brazil's three first-round matches. "I have not seen the present Brazilian team," confessed the Wales manager who had not seen Hungary, Mexico or Sweden either. "So from a tactical viewpoint I am flying a bit blind." Murphy's searches proved fruitless. The English party, including his good friend Winterbottom, had returned home before the Welsh had arrived in Kungälv. It was all so typical.

The second and biggest problem facing Murphy was the fitness of

John Charles, who had taken a hammering at the hands of
Hungary's defenders. Even with Charles in the side, Wales were
given little hope of beating Brazil. Without him, it would surely be a
slaughter.

The Welsh manager set the masseurs on Charles and another of
Hungary's victims, Hewitt. The latter was expected to recover in time
for the 7pm kick-off, but Charles was in extreme discomfort and the
most common question he was asked by the Press was, 'Are you
going to play?'

"It will take an army to stop me turning out against Brazil,"
responded the battered striker. "I am doing everything humanly
possible to be fit enough to play."

Murphy, the fine man-manager that he was, sensed Charles's
despondency as he began to lose his race against time. As Charles
received treatment from Jack Jones he tried to gee up his star player,
telling him, "You'll be fit, John! Don't worry, you'll be fit!" The
Juventus player, sensing the worst, just smiled back. "I knew I
wouldn't be fit," Charles admits today. "I was thinking during the
Hungary match, 'If we win this I won't be playing in the next game'. I
was in a bad way. I couldn't move my right leg and I couldn't walk. I
was in a hell of a lot of pain. The team doctor, Bill Hughes, said I
would be all right and that it was only a strain but it didn't improve.
If anything it got worse."

Murphy would wait until the eleventh hour before making a decision on Charles. "Jimmy had me out training," says Charles. "He got
me running, and I was running OK, but it hurt when I turned. I just
couldn't turn with my right leg. Everyone tried hard to get me fit –
Jack was rubbing my leg down all the time – but it was no good."

It was left to Charles to decide if he* could play. If he felt fit
enough, his name would be on the team-sheet. If not, then someone
else would take his place. "Not long before the kick-off I tried my leg
out again," explains Charles. "It was never going to be all right. I
couldn't jump either. I could do a standing jump, but I couldn't run
and jump. I told Jimmy I couldn't play, that my legs couldn't do it. If
I did play and I suffered another injury early on in the game I would
have been out altogether and we would have been down to 10 men. It
was better someone who was 100 per cent fit should play."

Charles confessed to his younger brother, Mel, that if he did play
he would let the side down. "John had a run-out in the morning," recalls Mel. "His legs were so swollen they looked like tree trunks. It
was clear by noon that there was no way he could play."

Murphy, with the 7pm kick-off on the horizon, received the news
he had been dreading – no John Charles. Now he had to find a

replacement, and there was no Trevor Ford, no Derek Tapscott and no Des Palmer. He could play Mel Charles in attack, but Mel, who had emerged as one of the best centre-backs in Sweden, would be needed to quell the formidable Brazilian attack.

Murphy, because of the chronic lack of strikers in the party of 18, was forced to pick Webster at centre-forward. The United player, even if it was only for 90 minutes, found himself removed from the Welsh FA's personae non gratae list. The selectors never forgave players for misbehaving and the Copacabana Club incident had almost certainly finished Webster's international career. In the foyer of the Grand Hotel the previous morning Webster came face-to-face with the selectors for the first time since the Verner Felt incident. "They didn't say anything but the expressions on their faces said I wouldn't play for Wales anymore," says Webster. The centre-forward joined Daniel and Ford on the Welsh FA's naughty boy list but because of circumstances in Gothenburg the selectors were forced to swallow their pride and play Webster one more time.

"Missing the Brazil match was the biggest disappointment of my career," reveals Charles. "I was very disappointed. In fact, I couldn't believe I would not play. It was devastating. But playing Colin was the right thing to do. I would have been useless." The injury turned out to be far worse than expected. Charles was sidelined for two months and missed the start of the 1958/59 Serie A season.

"Herbert Powell said I could go home if I wanted to because I was injured and no good to the team but I wanted to watch the Brazil match with Jimmy," says Charles. "It was absolute murder watching from the bench. Bloody murder!"

The news of Charles's absence upset the rest of the players. Medwin recalls, "We never realised his injury was that bad. Everyone thought it was just a knock and he would recover. John was very upset at the time. His heart and soul was in his country. That day when we played Brazil was the only time I've ever seen him upset. His eyes filled up."

Charles was probably the only Welsh player the Brazilians feared. Instead of using his immense height to batter the South American back four, the Gentle Giant would be sitting next to Murphy and Jack Jones on the bench. "John's absence boosted the Brazilians, no doubt about it. There were some long faces in the dressing room but Murphy made us forget John with his team-talk," says Hopkins. "To beat the Brazilians with John we'd have had to have played very well. To beat them without John we'd have to play exceptionally well. Losing him was big downer. After we beat Hungary to reach the quarter-finals we thought Brazil would be afraid of John Charles.

Now we didn't even have that. They weren't afraid of Ivor Allchurch or Terry Medwin or Cliff Jones even though they were good players. But they would be afraid of John because of the profile he had in Italy. Truthfully, I didn't think we'd win without John Charles."

Williams says Wales missed Charles for two reasons. "There was his height for crosses and he was an outlet because even though John was a big bloke he had good control. He could hold the ball up and bring other players into the game," explains the former West Bromwich Albion defender. "But we lost John's ability. It happened and we just had to get on with it. Sometimes when you lose your best player it lifts the other players by five per cent. Colin Webster was a different type of player to John. He gave 100 per cent but he didn't have John's qualities." Mel Charles agrees. "Brazil were over the moon John wasn't playing because they were no good in the air."

The moment the World Cup draw was made in Zürich in February, the Brazilians, managed by the studious Vicente Feola, were hot favourites. Whether they deserved this honour was open to question. Their European tour of 1956 had been unimpressive. They lost to England and Italy, drew with Czechoslovakia and Switzerland and just about beat Austria, Portugal and Turkey. They had looked lethargic in the qualifying games against Peru. It needed one of Didi's special *folha seca* free-kicks (*folha seca* means 'dry leaf' – the name given to Didi's deceptive swerving shots because he put so much spin on the ball it would hang and curl in the air like a leaf falling from a tree) to beat Peru in the crunch match in the Maracana.

When it came to individuals, Brazil had no equals. Apart from the midfield general Didi, who was known as the Black Cobra, there was Garrincha, the Little Bird, a fast, skillful right-winger who had a twisted right leg, the result of contracting polio as a child living in the impoverished mountain village of Pau Grande. Garrincha, despite his obvious ability, was no favourite of Feola who left him out of the first two games against Austria and England because of his poor defensive qualities. The 0–0 draw against the English worried the Brazilian players who felt their attack lacked flair. The players decided to lobby Feola for Garrincha's inclusion. Nilton Santos, the 32-year-old left-back, headed the deputation which convinced Feola to pick Garrincha ahead of the conservative Joel for the third match against Russia. Brazil were transformed and won 2–0. Garrincha would naturally start against the Welsh. With Garrincha on the right wing there was Mario Zagallo on the left. Zagallo was a completely different winger to Garrincha. He was more calculating, more European. He preferred to roam in midfield and make undetected runs into the opponent's penalty area.

In attack, the first-choice striker was 19-year-old José Alatafini. Like Garrincha, Altafini had incurred the wrath of Feola who felt the teenager's imminent big-money move to Milan had gone to his head. Altafini began the competition but was soon replaced by the giant, hawk-nosed Vavà. However, Vavà had been injured against the Soviet Union so the fair-haired Altafini was recalled into attack against Wales.

His partner was another teenager, 17-year-old Edson Arantes do Nascimento, otherwise known as Pelé. If Didi was the Black Cobra and Garrincha the Little Bird, Pelé was the Black Pearl. The son of a relatively unknown footballer, Dondinho, Pelé signed for Santos in 1956 and the following year made his international debut against Argentina. Good things were being said about Pelé, although he nearly missed out on the World Cup after injuring his knee in a league match against Corinthians shortly before the squad flew to Gothenburg. Like Garrincha, Pelé missed the first two games but was brought in against the Russians to shake-up the forward line. He did not disappoint. Before the Wales match Pelé was still considered a raw and unproven striker. He was certainly not the star of the side. That title belonged to Didi, but not for much longer.

Feola could also boast an iron-strong defence. At centre-half was the powerfully-built Bellini, the team's captain, at right-back the reliable Nilton De Sordi and at left-back Nilton Santos who had perfected the overlapping run. Gilmar, the goalkeeper, was the icing on the cake. Reputed to be the greatest goalkeeper Brazil has produced, he also had a legitimate claim in 1958 of being the world number one.

"In my opinion," says Hopkins, "the Brazilian team that played in Sweden was the best Brazilian side of all, better than the one in 1970 in Mexico. They were all great players. They were a brilliant team. They had a brilliant attack, a brilliant midfield, a brilliant defence and also a brilliant goalkeeper." Hopkins has a point. In reaching the last eight Brazil, had scored five but, more significantly, conceded none.

According to the pundits the Brazil-Wales quarter-final was, out of the four, the easiest to call. It would be a Brazilian victory, and a comfortable one at that. For the Welsh it would be their third game in five days, a punishing schedule even for the fittest of teams. Only 48 hours earlier, on a warm evening in Stockholm, they had pushed themselves to the limit against Hungary. They were also without John Charles and, as Group Three runners-up, they had been forced to travel to Gothenburg from Stockholm. Surely in the Nya Ullevi Stadium they would succumb not only to the dazzling skills of Brazil but also to physical and mental exhaustion. Feola remained cautious despite the avalanche of predictions forecasting a handsome Brazil win. "No team that can draw with Hungary once and then beat them a second time can be taken lightly," he warned.

The day before the match both teams used the Nya Ullevi for warming-up sessions. Wales were first. "The Brazilians came to watch us train," says Webster, who had missed the previous two matches against Sweden and Hungary. "We were lapping around the pitch and we could see the Brazilian players shaking their heads in disbelief. They thought we were mad. After nine months of playing football there we were running around the pitch. When we finished we watched them warm-up. They all had a ball each. They didn't do any running. Everything they did was with the ball. They'd start off with 22 balls, then it would go down to 11, then six, then just one."

The Brazil squad of 1958 was the most prepared the World Cup had seen. Every eventuality was covered and the quarter-final in Gothenburg became not just a battle between Brazil and Wales but also a battle between the best-prepared side in Sweden and the worst.

As well as the usual trainer, doctors and masseurs, the Brazilian FA also flew over a psychologist, dentists, a chef and their own food. The head of the medical team, Dr Hilton Gosling, spent an entire month touring Sweden in 1957 searching for the perfect base for Feola and his players. Gosling visited 25 possible headquarters, meticulously assessing each one. He plumped for the Turisthotellet in Hindas, around 35 miles from Gothenburg. With only 500 inhabitants, Hindas, encased by lakes and forests, guaranteed the Brazilians privacy.

Feola was helped in team selection by João Carvalhaes, a psychologist from Sao Paolo. Carvalhaes had the task of weeding out any players who were motivated by money rather than love of their country. He also chose what music should be played in the hotel and banned the players from receiving letters and reading newspapers. Carvalhaes also conducted tests to decide which 11 players were mentally prepared for World Cup football.

Interestingly, had the psychologist had his way neither Garrincha nor Pelé would have played against Wales. Garrincha had dismally failed one of the psychologist's mental tests, scoring 38 out of 123, while Carvalhaes described Pelé as infantile, lacking in fighting spirit and not having the responsibility to understand team spirit. Feola decided to ignore the advice.

"One newspaper said we would lose by five or six goals," remembers Hewitt. "We didn't have any time to prepare for the game but it didn't really matter. We had just played nine months of league football and we were as fit as fiddles. We weren't tired, we were full of it. I don't know about the others but I couldn't wait to get onto the pitch. We knew it was going to be hard but we also had some world-class players. I'm convinced Brazil were a little scared of us. We had a great goalkeeper and two First Division full-backs."

Just as the preparations and the style of football between the two nations were different, so too were the managers. The only thing Feola and Murphy had in common was physical appearance. Both were short, stocky men in late middle age but there the similarities ended. As Hopkins describes him, Murphy was "one of the lads". He enthusiastically took part in five and six-a-side games, let the players indulge in the odd beer and cigarette (Murphy himself was a drinker and smoker) and, regardless of form, he always picked the star players – Kelsey, Allchurch, Jones and John Charles. He was also more of a motivator, not a tactician. In contrast, Feola viewed football as a science and kept files on every match he watched. He was a tactical innovator, developing the 4–2–4 formation, and he was more detached from his players than Murphy. He had no respect for reputations and dropped players if he felt they were not contributing to the *seleçao*, shown with the way he dealt with Garrincha and later Altafini. Feola even threatened to leave Didi at home, claiming he was not working hard enough.

"I am not going to say we will beat the Brazilians but, by gum, we are going to make a mighty effort to do so," said Murphy. "I have every confidence in my own defence but it looks as though the Brazilian rearguard is going to take a bit of cracking." The night before the quarter-final, Murphy, in his room in the Fars Hatt Hotel, thought hard about his team's strategy for the Brazil game. Still "flying blind" he decided on the same approach he took with the Swedes and adopted Herbert Chapman's 4–2–4 approach used at Arsenal two decades earlier.

The eleven men who would face Brazil were: Kelsey, Williams, Hopkins, Sullivan, Mel Charles, Bowen, Medwin, Hewitt, Webster, Allchurch, Jones. The only change from the play-off match was, of course, Webster for Charles. The beanpole-like Hopkins had the job of watching Garrincha, Williams would mark Zagallo, Charles would stick close to Altafini, Sullivan would mark Pelé, and Bowen had the toughest job of the lot – to staunch the Brazilian attacks by snuffing out Didi.

"We played a defensive game," admits Williams who had an excellent World Cup. "Our plan was to frustrate them and then hopefully catch them on the break. If we could keep a clean sheet, make two or three breakaway chances and take one of them, that would be enough."

The four quarter-finals, Northern Ireland-France in Norrköping, West Germany-Yugoslavia in Malmö, Sweden-Soviet Union in Stockholm and Brazil-Wales in Gothenburg, kicked-off at the same time – 7pm on Thursday, June 19. Brazil, West Germany, France and Sweden were tipped to reach the last four.

With just minutes to go before the players were called into the Nya Ullevi's tunnel, Murphy delivered his most inspiring dressing-room speech yet. Those who were present remember it well. "He just rubbished the Brazilians," smiles Williams. "He said they were vastly overrated and that they were not all they were cracked up to be. He said we were just like them – we had two hands and two feet." John Charles, dressed in casual clothing, stood next to Murphy as he delivered his pep talk. "He said Pelé couldn't play, Didi couldn't play," laughs Charles. "He had a go at every one of their players. He said there was a boy in the Manchester United junior team who was better than Garrincha. Jimmy had the ability of giving confidence to his players. The lads were nine feet tall when they left the dressing-room."

The skies above Gothenburg were overcast that evening. The attendance, once again, was disappointing. The futuristic Ullevi held 51,500 but the crowd was nearly half that at 25,923. Live television coverage of the Sweden-Soviet Union clash was blamed for the low gate. Bowen, for the second game in succession, won the toss and chose to play the first-half with a light breeze behind Wales.

Now, for the first time, the Welsh defenders saw their opponents in the flesh – Garrincha, Pelé, Didi, Zagallo. No longer were they names. They were real men, limbering up and wearing the famous canary yellow jersey of Brazil. "Garrincha was a freak," says Hopkins. "I looked at him and saw that his legs went the wrong way. One of his legs was bent in. I thought, 'How's he going to get past me with legs like that?' But his footwork was so quick. How he didn't fall over I don't know. He had balance, he was small, he was quick and he could hit a ball as well."

The Austrian referee Erich Seipelt got the match underway. The crowd were anticipating a samba show from the first minute until the last but to their astonishment it was Wales who launched the first serious attacks. After five minutes play, Jones zipped past De Sordi and crossed into the penalty area where Webster was waiting. With just Gilmar to beat, it was a glorious chance, but Charles's deputy hastily fired into the side-netting. A few minutes later Webster spurned another opportunity, this time from a Medwin cross, but the ball just shaved the top of his head. After those two raids the South Americans lay siege to Kelsey's goalmouth.

"I would love to have had those chances again," sighs Webster. "If I was a bit taller I would probably have scored from Terry Medwin's cross. I was only five feet seven." He is not bothered by the inevitable talk that Charles would have scored from the few opportunities Wales created that night. "At least I got into the positions. John Charles may not have done. John didn't really live up to expectations in Sweden. Ivor turned out to be our best player. I couldn't get much past Santos and Bellini. They were playing as if they were on a beach but we created more chances against Brazil than any other side. We just didn't have the luck that day."

It was Wales, not Brazil, who controlled the first 20 minutes with Sullivan, Bowen and Allchurch emerging as the dominant figures. "When I saw Colin miss those chances," says Charles, "I couldn't help think to myself that I would have put them away. I turned to Jimmy and said, 'I would have scored that'. Still, I thought all the lads played heroically that day." His brother Mel adds, "We could have been 2–0 up. What could you expect from Colin? He was only a small bloke. He did all he could in the match but only he would deny he wasn't as good as John." Ken Jones, however, praises Webster's contribution. "He did well, Colin. He was a busy little player, very hard to handle. He did very well against Brazil."

The reason for Wales's early pressure was the form of the two wingers, Jones and Medwin. Jones was giving De Sordi a hard time while Medwin was causing the great Nilton Santos problems. "Terry and myself got in more crosses against Brazil than we did in the other four matches put together," remarks Jones. "De Sordi was great in possession, but I found him a little slow on the turn. He wasn't a problem like Bergmark was. He wasn't a good defender. We caused their defence quite a few problems and if Big John was playing I'm sure there would have been a sensational result."

With the halfway mark in the first-half approaching Feola's team started to take over. Pelé dribbled through the Welsh defence but Kelsey, his hands sticky with chewing gum, robbed the ball from his lightning quick toes. Then the Arsenal goalkeeper had to deal with a series of fierce shots, from Didi, Garrincha and Pelé again.

Zagallo then created Brazil's best chance so far. For the first time, he rounded Williams and crossed into the Welsh penalty area but Altafini volleyed wide. This was the start of a miserable night for Altafini who found himself shackled by Mel Charles. Of all the young Brazilian players in Sweden it was Altafini who found himself burdened with high expectations, no doubt fuelled by his imminent £80,000 move from Palmeiras to Milan. Against Wales he had a chance to take back his place from Vavà but, thanks to the Swansea

Town defender, he failed dismally. After this quarter-final Altafini would never play for Brazil again. "He suited me because he wasn't a ball player," says Mel Charles. "He was more of an English centre-forward. He was good in the air, but against me he had no chance in the air and he didn't see much of the play. Altafini started losing his confidence and whenever he got the ball he couldn't control it." Mel's performance against Brazil, and especially the way he shackled Altafini, cemented his name in the 1958 World Cup XI team. It was ironic that before the World Cup, it was his older brother John who dominated the headlines. After it, it was Mel who made the prestigious XI. Pelé, too, lavished him with praise, picking him as the best centre-half in Sweden. "You can't get a better compliment than that, can you?" he smiles.

Wales had survived to half-time. The giant scoreboard perched on the Nya Ullevi read 0–0. The Welsh left the field to a round of applause. As for the Brazilians, it had been anti-climax. They headed for the dressing-room concerned, puzzled, anxious. When the half-time score from Gothenburg was confirmed there were gasps of astonishment from the crowds at the other three quarter-final venues. During the 1958 World Cup, the scores from all the matches played at the same time were displayed within each ground.

"John Charles came into the dressing-room and said to us, 'We can beat them!' It was a quarter-final match – anything could happen," says Webster. "Jimmy Murphy said to carry on what we were doing in the first-half but this time do it even better. The truth was we couldn't do anymore."

The crowd sensed an upset. Brazil had struggled to prise open the Welsh rearguard while the men in red had created a couple of good chances. Was Murphy's plan going to pay off once more?

Wales started the second-half just as they did the first, on the attack. Now Medwin was at the heart of everything good. First, he beat Santos and forced a fine save from Gilmar with a fierce, angled shot. Then he whipped another tantalising cross into the Brazilian penalty area but Webster was flagged off-side. "We kept harassing them. Jimmy told us not to let them settle," remarks Medwin. "It was a cup match, a one-off, so we fancied our chances even though we were considered lambs to the slaughter."

Then, after quarter-of-an hour, the tide turned. Brazil, with Didi as the orchestrator, launched attack after attack, but every single one broke down by the time they reached the Welsh penalty area. Wales's iron defence stood firm. Bowen, the inspirational captain, urged his team-mates on. His voice could be heard from the Ullevi's stands. "Get into them lads! Don't let them settle on the ball!" Bowen was

Murphy's trusted lieutenant. Murphy drew up the blueprint for victory and Bowen ensured it was religiously carried out on the field.

"I tried to make Garrincha go outside me and down the wing," explains Hopkins, who marked the Brazilian winger that evening with considerable success. "If he did go down the wing I could get a sliding tackle in because I was quick. I think I did quite well against him." Cliff Jones adds, "That day Mel gave the best display I've ever seen from a full-back. He didn't give Garrincha a kick. He dictated which way he should go. Mel was awkward to play against because he had these long legs."

Williams, who completely shut out Zagallo, recalls Murphy's instructions to his defenders. "The plan was to draw them in and make them play the ball into places they didn't want to play. We worked on the principle that goals were scored inside the area, so we defended the edge of the penalty box to stop them getting behind us. The wing-halves would cover back as well. If I went to stop Zagallo, Derrick Sullivan would cover behind me. When Mel was dealing with Garrincha, Dave Bowen would cover behind him."

Against Wales, Zagallo, who would manage the World Cup winning side in 1970 in Mexico, and the side which finished second in 1998 in France, had arguably his quietest 90 minutes of the tournament. "I found him quite straightforward," explains Williams. "He was a bit like Gento of Spain. He wanted to play one-twos or push the ball past you, but I was quick in those days and I could match him for speed."

On the few occasions the Welsh defence were beaten, Kelsey was on hand to put out the flames. He had played a splendid match against Sweden, but against Brazil the Arsenal goalkeeper surpassed himself. "Jack had a wonderful game," says Ken Jones, the reserve goalkeeper who watched the quarter-final from the bench with Murphy and John Charles. "People talk about Gordon Banks's save against Pelé. Well, Jack made three saves of that calibre from Didi. Jack was a brave goalkeeper and a good reader of the game. He cut out a lot of danger before it happened. He was very commanding and his contribution to our World Cup campaign was tremendous. Personally, he wasn't my favourite person, but you had to admire him."

The Gothenburg quarter-final then entered the last 20 minutes. With Feola's side beginning to run out of ideas it looked as if extra-time was looming. "They became very, very frustrated," recalls Williams. "We could see them starting to fall out with one other and that spurned us on. Altafini, I remember, was really getting annoyed with the service he was receiving." The young Brazilian, closely marked by Mel Charles, had lost his self-control and Seipelt booked him for a foul on Bowen. "They were probably over-confident and the longer the match went on the less likely it seemed Brazil would score. They became frustrated and resorted to long-range shots," adds Williams.

After Medwin's early effort, Wales hardly tested Gilmar in the second-half. Most of the game was played in the Welsh half, around Kelsey's penalty area. "The attacks were coming from everywhere, especially from Santos at full-back," says Hopkins. "They were all good footballers. They could all attack. Possession-wise, it was very one-sided. We defended well but if anyone was going to score it was them."

There were just 17 minutes left when Pelé, standing near the penalty-spot and shadowed by Mel Charles, brilliantly controlled Didi's header. Didi made his way into the area looking for the return pass but Pelé decided to go it alone. With lightning speed he turned Charles and lined up a shot. Williams came in to block just as Pelé connected. It was a feeble strike but the ball scraped the underneath of Williams's boot and rolled past the horrified Kelsey who was rooted to the ground. The ball sat in the right-hand corner of the net. At last, Brazil had broken the deadlock. Pelé, screaming "Gooooooooaaaaaalllllll!" and with tears in his eyes, ran into the net and kissed the ball. It was his first World Cup goal. He would later describe it as the most important, and the luckiest, he has ever scored.

The Brazilian team celebrated inside Kelsey's goal. They had piled on top of Pelé just as they did with Vavà in the Soviet Union match. The Welsh players stood still in disbelief. Some, like Williams, had their hands on their heads. Others, like Bowen, had their hands on their hips. Hopkins, a forlorn figure, walked into the net and fought his way through the mass of yellow shirts to grab the ball. There was little more than quarter-of-an-hour left to snatch an unlikely equaliser. Webster recalls the scenes after Pelé's lucky strike. "I've never seen so many people inside the net. They were relieved. They were bloody relieved. I felt sick. I thought we had a chance of winning."

The Welsh bench was distraught. As John Charles remembers, "Jimmy was devastated. He called Pelé a 'black bastard' after he scored. He said to me, 'After all this we're going to lose'. I really felt for him."

Afterwards, Kelsey said Pelé's shot only beat him because it took a slight, but nevertheless crucial, deflection. Had it not hit Williams's boot, he would have saved it. "Jack would say that," smiles Williams, who was a close friend of Kelsey. "But I came in from the right, so if I had deflected it, the ball would have gone closer to Jack, not away from him."

The former right-back remembers the Brazilian goal as if it were yesterday and he has no regrets trying to stop Pelé's shot. "He was in the box. I was covering. He beat one of our defenders and I could see he was going to shoot. I dived in to block but I was a split-second too late. The ball caught my studs. I felt a quiver underneath my right boot. It wasn't an obvious deflection. If only I'd got there a split-second earlier I would have blocked it. I didn't feel responsible for the goal. I was doing a covering job. You have to give Pelé credit. That's where he was so good. He controlled the ball and hit it so quickly. It gave the goalkeeper no chance. Jack wasn't expecting the shot."

Ken Jones agrees with Williams. Kelsey, with or without a deflection, had little hope of saving the shot, even though it was hit tamely. "It was a melee in the goalmouth. There were so many players in the box at the time. I think there were nine players all within a few yards of the ball. That situation is a nightmare for a goalkeeper. You just hope one of the defenders can block any shot."

In the final minutes Brazil played possession football and, visibly relaxed, even performed a few party tricks. Altafini finally escaped Mel Charles but his header hit the bar. It ended 1–0. Brazil would march on to the semi-final in Stockholm. Wales, despite their gallant display, would fly home to watch the remainder of the tournament on television.

While Feola's men sportingly paraded the Swedish flag on a lap of honour around the Nya Ullevi pitch the Welsh players were applauded off the field.

The Welsh dressing-room ached with the pain of defeat. Nobody had expected them to beat Brazil, but to have conceded such a soft goal after holding the Brazilians for more than 70 minutes obviously affected Murphy's players. "I felt terrible," says Mel Charles. "If it was a great goal I wouldn't have complained, but it wasn't. I can still see it today – it was like a golf putt." Webster adds, "We all felt gutted. We were so near. Murphy was delighted with our performance. He said we had done our country proud. He knew we gave everything. We were down but not for long. It was only a game." Hewitt recalls, "The dressing-room was very quiet afterwards. Everyone was upset. Jimmy Murphy praised us for putting up such a good show and patted us all on the back. I know we got beat but we did a good job."

Judging from the comments made by some of the Brazilian players, it seemed the South Americans had underestimated Wales. "You people tried to fool us," Didi told reporters after the game. "We had been told that Wales was the weakest of the countries in Britain, and that we could take things easy. Instead of that, we found ourselves up against a team full of fight and yet, although they tackled strongly, they never tackled illegally."

In the other quarter-finals, France thrashed Northern Ireland 4–0, although the scoreline was influenced by several Irish players, notably Gregg in goal and Casey at inside-right, nursing injuries. Doherty's team also had to make an eight-hour coach journey to Norrköping from their first-round base at Tylösand which was 210 miles away. Wisnieski, Fontaine (twice) and Piantoni scored the goals. In Stockholm the hosts ensured their place in the last four by soundly beating the Soviet Union 2–0 with goals from Hamrin and Simonsson while in Malmö the holders, West Germany, beat Yugoslavia with a winner from Rahn. The three play-off teams not only failed to win their quarter-final matches, they also failed to score a single goal between them. For the next World Cup, in Chile, FIFA scrapped the play-off system in favour of goal difference.

The semi-finals, held on June 24, were Brazil-France in Stockholm and Sweden-West Germany in Gothenburg. In the best match of series Brazil beat France 5–2 with goals from Vavà, Didi and a hat-trick from Pelé. France replied through Fontaine and Piantoni. Sweden beat the holders 3–1. Rahn put the Germans ahead but the hosts came back with goals from Skoglund, Gren and Hamrin.

The final was held on June 29, in Stockholm's Rasunda Stadium. Brazil became the first team to win the World Cup on a different continent, beating Sweden 5–2. To the delight of the 49,757 crowd Liedholm gave the Swedes the lead after four minutes. Raynor made two bold predictions in the 1958 competition. The first, that Sweden would reach the final. The second, that Brazil would panic if they conceded the first goal. He was proved right with the first but spectacularly wrong with the second. After Liedholm's strike, Brazil hit five through Vavà and Pelé, who both scored twice, and Zagallo.

"The matches they played after us shows how good that result against Wales was," says Medwin. "They put five past France and five past Sweden. But against us they could only score one." In 1962, a few months before the World Cup in Chile, Brazil decided to play two warm-up matches. They chose Wales as opponents. According to Ken Jones, "Ever since that quarter-final in 1958 the Brazilians have had a respect for Welsh football, and it has lasted to this day."

In his autobiography, *My Life and the Beautiful Game*, Pelé recalled the Brazil-Wales quarter-final. "Nobody really believed Wales could give us much trouble, and with all the praise we received from the newspapers and the other media I'm afraid we began to believe it ourselves. Confidence is good, even necessary, but over-confidence can be a dangerous thing. We went back to the Nya Ullevi Stadium convinced we had nothing to worry about and that the game would be an easy warm-up for whoever we would be called upon to face in the semi-finals. Possibly because of this over-confidence – or just possibly because the Welsh team had been greatly underrated, despite the newspaper articles – we found ourselves in the toughest struggle of the entire tournament so far. "

Their World Cup adventure over, the Welsh squad returned to the Fars Hatt Hotel where Murphy gave them permission to drown their sorrows. The following day, on three different flights, the Welsh contingent would fly back to London Airport.

Murphy later claimed Wales would have beaten Brazil had John Charles been playing. Most of the players agree with the late manager. Cliff Jones says, "Against Brazil, Terry Medwin and myself played our best games. We got some good crosses in at the far post. Colin Webster was a good player but there was only one John Charles. I'm certain that had John been playing that day he would have got on the end of those crosses and made them count." Mel Charles goes even further. "I think we could have gone all the way to the final. I'm not being biased, but we had class in Ivor, Cliffie, Terry and John. We would have won against Brazil with John in the team. He was great in the air, they weren't."

There was no welcome party for the Welsh squad when they arrived in London on June 20. The players simply made their own way home from the airport. Cliff Jones, Medwin, Hopkins, Kelsey and Bowen, the Arsenal and Tottenham players, made the relatively short trip to north London. Sullivan, Baker, Hewitt, Ken Jones, Mel Charles and Allchurch, the Cardiff and Swansea players, caught the train to South Wales. They were joined by Webster, who was returning home to Cardiff for a week before heading back to Manchester. John Charles had flown to the Italian Riviera to recover from the injuries sustained in the play-off while the rest of the squad broke up – Williams and Crowe to the West Midlands, Vernon to Blackburn, Leek to Northampton.

"Nothing was said, nothing was done," says Hewitt, one of the many players disappointed with the country's apathetic response. "It was a bit of a let-down really. I was surprised and disappointed no-one organised a do for us. It was very poor. It would have been lovely to have an open-top coach ride in Cardiff." Webster recalls arriving at Cardiff Central with the Cardiff City players. "Nobody knew who we were. I jumped into a taxi and went to my mother's house in Ely. When I arrived she said to me, 'Hello Colin, I didn't know you were coming home today. Do you want a cup of tea?'" Mel Charles had an unusual welcome when he stepped off the train at Swansea. "The ticket conductor saw me with my case and said, 'Been on your holidays again, Mel?' And we had just played in the World Cup quarter-finals. I don't suppose he had been reading the papers."

CHAPTER TWELVE

FORTY YEARS ON

JUNE 19, 1998. It is exactly 40 years since Wales's last World Cup match. Of the eleven players who faced Brazil in Gothenburg seven are alive to celebrate the anniversary – Mel Charles, Cliff Jones, Ron Hewitt, Terry Medwin, Mel Hopkins, Stuart Williams and Colin Webster.

Mel Charles lives alone in a flat in Uplands, Swansea. He is 63. Like most of the surviving members of the 1958 squad the ex-defender is retired. He was a wanted man after Sweden. In 1959 he left Swansea Town for Arsenal. "I didn't want to leave Swansea," he says. "Tottenham, Chelsea and Arsenal wanted to sign me. I accepted Arsenal. They were offering Swansea £47,000 which was the lowest figure of the three. I thought Swansea would turn it down and I would stay, but they didn't." Mel was on his way to Highbury where he played not at centre-half but centre-forward. "I didn't like it at Arsenal. There were all Scots, English and Irish there. They didn't mix. It wasn't a friendly place and I had come from Swansea which was very close-knit."

In 1962, after several injuries and run-ins with the Arsenal manager, George Swindin, he returned to Wales to join Cardiff City. He was ousted from the team when City signed his brother, John, from Roma in 1965. Mel ended his career with Portmadoc, Port Vale and Haverfordwest. "I loved playing for Portmadoc and Haverfordwest. There was no pressure. I really enjoyed my football."

Outside football, Mel tried his hand at several business ventures. He opened a scrap company, a wholesale potato business and a butcher shop. Like his brother, Mel discovered he was not blessed with an entrepreneur's mind. "The potato business finished when I was in Mauritius," he explains. "I was over there playing with the John Charles XI. We were only supposed to stay out there for two weeks but we ended up staying for five because it was beautiful. When I came back all the potatoes had run out. The butcher shop closed while I was away on the Isle of Wight for a month. A holiday camp wanted me to go there and teach people how to head the ball."

Cliff Jones lives in Cheshunt, Hertfordshire. He is 63 and a part-time games instructor with Islington Borough Council. After Sweden, his career continued to go from strength to strength. Jones became a key member of Bill Nicholson's all-conquering Tottenham side. 'Cliffie' was part of the 'double' team of 1961. He also won the FA Cup in 1962, the Cup Winners Cup in 1963 and, as a substitute, the FA Cup for a third time in 1967. In 1968, he joined Fulham on a free transfer.

Like Mel Charles, Jones had a bad experience with a butcher shop. He opened one in 1965, in the shadow of Tottenham's White Hart Lane ground. It closed three years later. "If there's one thing I learned in business, it's that you must know what's going on, how you're doing and what your stock is. I didn't know any of these things. But I didn't go bankrupt. I used the £8,000 I received from joining Fulham to pay everyone off."

Jones joined Fulham when a young Bobby Robson was manager. "He said he was going to get us out of Division Two and he did – into Division Three!" After little more than one season at Craven Cottage the winger was on his way. He played for Kings Lynn, Wealdstone, Bedford Town, Cambridge City and Wingate before retiring from football at 42. He joined Islington Borough Council as a games instructor in 1972 and works at Highbury Grove Comprehensive. He went part-time in 1993. "The great thing about it is that it keeps me in shape. The only problem is that it's in Arsenal territory," he laughs. "I may retire. When I'm 65 I'll see what happens."

Ron Hewitt lives in a flat in Wrexham, about a mile from The Racecourse ground. He is 70 and retired five years ago. After the quarter-final against Brazil, Hewitt never played for Wales again. In 1959, he re-joined Wrexham from Cardiff City, then he moved to Coventry City and finally Chester. Like so many of the 1958 team, Hewitt played non-league football, with Witton Albion, Caernarfon Town and Barmouth.

Then he emigrated to Australia. "I had a phone call from Sydney, from a club called Bankstown. They offered me a two-year contract. I asked my wife if she wanted to go and she agreed. Her mother died and we saw it as a new start." But after two years the Hewitts returned. "I could have stayed out there – nice people, nice climate. But my wife didn't like it." Hewitt took a job as a fitter with BICC, a cable company in Wrexham, where he worked until 1993. "I'm having a nice, comfortable retirement. I've always been careful with money. I wasn't a spendthrift. I would like to have coached, especially when you see what's happening today. I would like to have carried on Cullis's methods."

Two of the 1958 squad, Mel Hopkins and Stuart Williams, have settled on the South Coast. Mel Hopkins lives in a flat in the seaside town of Shoreham-by-Sea, just a few miles outside Brighton. Now 64, he took early retirement in March 1998 when the sports centre he worked in at nearby Horsham closed down.

Hopkins was a mainstay of Bill Nicholson's Tottenham team, but a horrific injury in 1959, while playing for Wales against Scotland in Glasgow, cost Hopkins a cabinet full of medals. "I was jumping for a corner when Ian St John accidentally headed me in the face. My nose completely shattered. There were pieces of nose bone falling out for weeks after that." He needed three operations to repair his nose and it meant he missed Tottenham's 'double' season in 1960/61. By the time he was ready to return to action Hopkins found his place taken by Ron Henry. "There was no way Nicholson was going to change a winning team. The injury cost me a league medal, two FA Cup medals and a Cup Winners Cup medal. It couldn't have come at a worse time." Hopkins has never seen St John since their clash of heads 39 years ago. In 1964 Hopkins joined Brighton in Division Four and helped them win the Division Four championship. He later starred for Bradford Park Avenue and Irish side Ballymena. "The Ballymena thing didn't last long. I was flying to Ireland every Friday from Gatwick. After a couple of months I'd had enough."

In 1974 he taught physical education in schools across Brighton before taking a job at a sports centre run by Horsham District Council. "Retirement is marvellous. I still do golf, swimming and cycling. I enjoy the South Coast. I like Sussex. It's a nice county to live in. I like going home to the Valleys now and again but I couldn't live there. It's changed so much."

Stuart Williams is still working at 68. To use his own words, he is a 'general dogsbody' for an import/export company in Southampton where he lives. "I can't afford to retire," he says. Williams left West Bromwich Albion in 1962. Then he joined Southampton and was a member of the team that won promotion to Division One in 1966. At 35 he retired from football to coach. He was youth-team coach at Albion, then first-team coach, but he left The Hawthorns after falling out with the chairman, Jimmy Gaunt. He then sold tools for a small engineering company in Birmingham before returning to football in 1970, to help his friend and former Wales team-mate Vic Crowe, who had taken charge of Aston Villa. "We were struggling at the bottom of Division Two at the time and despite all our efforts we went down."

He then became manager of a club in Tehran called Paykaan, in Abadan. However, in a fit of pique, Paykaan's multi-millionaire owner disbanded the club following a row over a cup competition. "He called me into his office and said he was getting rid of the team, just like that." Williams then headed for Norway, where he led Stavanger to the championship in 1974. In 1976 he returned to Southampton as assistant manager. In recent years he has worked as a rep for a tyre company and a clerk for a transport firm.

Terry Medwin lives in West Cross, Swansea. The man who scored Wales's only winning goal in the World Cup is 66. Medwin retired in 1983 after suffering a nervous illness which first surfaced in 1980, while he was John Toshack's assistant at high-flying Swansea City. Seventeen years later Medwin, after psychiatric treatment, is still recovering from the illness.

The winger had his fair share of bad luck after the 1958 competition. Two years later, while Wales were playing Scotland at Ninian Park, Medwin's father, who was at the game watching his son, suffered a heart attack and later died in hospital. Medwin sensed something awful had happened while he was playing after hearing the loudspeakers announce his brother-in-law's name. Then in 1960, just five weeks before the season started, Medwin fell ill with a mystery bug. Terry Dyson replaced him for the first match, against Everton. Tottenham won 2–0 and Dyson became first-choice in a season which saw Tottenham win the 'double'. Medwin managed to make 14 appearances, enough to earn him a league winners' medal, but he missed the FA Cup final against Leicester City. "I wasn't happy, but you have to go along with it," he says. "Terry was playing well."

Medwin won the FA Cup with Tottenham in 1962 but a year later his career came to an abrupt end when he broke his leg in three places while playing in a pre-season tour of South Africa. It happened in Cape Town, in the first minute of the first match against the South African national team. In 1965 he was forced to quit. Medwin turned to coaching, first with non-league Cheshunt, then as reserve team coach at Cardiff City in 1967, and first-team coach at Fulham in 1969. Seven years later he became Norwich City's reserve-team coach. According to the softly-spoken Medwin, his two years at Carrow Road were the happiest since his playing days. "It was a nice quality of life. It's better to be an assistant with a First or Second Division club than manager of a club struggling in Division Four."

In 1978 Toshack invited Medwin to become his number two. Medwin agreed. "The only reason I agreed was because it would mean coming back to Swansea." Toshack and Medwin masterminded the Swans' meteoric rise up the league ladder. Then, on

December 27, 1980, after a nailbiting 3–3 draw with rivals Cardiff City at Ninian Park, Medwin started to feel unwell. "I don't know what happened to me. It was something to do with nerves, but not a nervous breakdown. It just came on, straight after the game with Cardiff. I'd played in the FA Cup final and the World Cup and I'd never been nervous. But all of a sudden I became fearful of everything."

Medwin had to relinquish his post and was offered a scouting job at The Vetch. That proved too much as well, and in 1983, Medwin stopped working. "I saw a psychiatrist. He said I had agoraphobia (a fear of open spaces). Sometimes I would wake up and sit on the end of my bed for 10 minutes just to get my bearings. I would have a mild depression. Maybe it was a late reaction to things that had happened to me before. For 10 years I had no zest for life. I just can't explain it. People would come and see me and I wouldn't look at them. I would see a specialist and tell him all my problems. They were silly things, but when you're not well they seem bad. I would come out from his office feeling a million dollars but an hour later I was back to square one. I never drank shorts and all of a sudden I was drinking two or three brandies a day. When the effect of the alcohol wore off I felt 10 times worse. It's not completely gone. I'd say I'm 80 per cent OK, but some days I still get this depression."

Despite his problems Medwin has built up a retirement nest-egg for him and his wife. Today he spends most of his time doting over his 18 grandchildren.

Colin Webster lives in Sketty, Swansea, opposite Singleton Park. The man who was once known as 'the Bad Boy of Welsh Football' is 66. As expected, the Copacabana Club incident killed off Webster's international career. It also threatened his career at Old Trafford. A week after returning from Sweden the Manchester United striker discovered he was on the transfer list. "Busby said I was letting the club down," says Webster. First there had been his tackle on Bolton's Dennis Stevens in the FA Cup final, then the fracas with the Mexicans followed by the headbutt in Soltsjöbaden. For the strict Busby, that was enough. "I pleaded with him for a second chance and he gave it to me." However, there was no comeback for Webster after he was sent off against Young Boys of Berne, in September 1958. Arthur Ellis ordered Webster off the pitch for retaliation.

Webster left Manchester for Swansea Town. After five fruitful seasons he was off to Newport County before finishing with Worcester City, Merthyr Tydfil and Portmadoc. "That bloke Ravanelli made more in one season than I did in 19 years of football," adds Webster. "The best money I earned was at Worcester, £40-a-week plus £2.50 for each goal." After football he made a living from scaffolding and he eventually ran his own company, Scafftex, but he closed the company in the 1970s following a slump. He later worked for an electrical company in Bridgend before working as a parks ranger in Swansea. He is now retired. "I could do with more money. I never had a testimonial. I never even got a bonus for the FA Cup final because we lost. My wife's a hairdresser, so that helps. We make ends meet because we have to."

The most famous member of the squad, John Charles, is 66. He lives in Birkenshaw, just outside Bradford, in a semi-detached council house. If any of the 1958 team ought to be living their last years in relative luxury it should be Big John. He made a fortune in Italy, but thanks to an expensive divorce and a clutch of failed businesses, that fortune disappeared long ago. He stayed at Juventus until 1962, then he signed for Leeds, Roma, Cardiff City, Hereford United (as player-manager) and Merthyr Tydfil (manager).

Charles lost money with several ventures – a restaurant in Turin, a sports shop in Cardiff and a baby clothes store in Leeds, which he opened with his second wife, Glenda. "I didn't do too much wrong in football, but in business it was a different story. I've made a hell of a lot of mistakes. It was hard to find custom for the sports shop and the baby clothes shop was the biggest blunder I made. It wasn't the right thing for me and it just slipped away."

Charles and his first wife, Peggy, divorced in 1977. "It hit me hard financially. It was half and half, and she wanted half." Then, with his second wife, he ran a hotel in Leeds. Again, the business venture ended unhappily. "The rent kept going up and up. In the end we couldn't afford it." Charles faced a 60 day prison term for failing to pay the hotel's debts but he was saved at the eleventh hour when Glenda came up with the money. Today, Charles is happy just watching Leeds play at Elland Road. He also does a spot of after-dinner speaking and is president of the ex-Leeds United Players Association. "People who say I should be a millionaire make me laugh. I never made enough money in Italy to live on for the rest of my life."

Four of the 1958 first-team have since died – Jack Kelsey, Dave Bowen, Ivor Allchurch and Derrick Sullivan. Sullivan stayed at Ninian Park until 1961 before moving to Exeter City. A year later he had signed for his hometown club, Newport County. 'Sulli' finished his career with Hereford United and Ebbw Vale. After hanging up his boots he followed in his father's footsteps and worked at Newport Docks, but Sullivan's heavy drinking finally caught up with him and in 1983, at the age of 53, he died. "No matter where we were, if the manager wasn't looking Derrick would have a pint of beer," recalls his friend and former Cardiff City team-mate, Ron Stitfall. "Derrick lived for the day and he liked a drink. He would come back from the summer looking like a little pig and it was not until November that he would get his fitness back. He was a natural. He had control, good passing, but he wasted his career. He could have been a Division One defender but he enjoyed his life outside football."

Jack Kelsey died in 1992, aged 62. He was forced to retire from football after injuring his back in a friendly against Brazil, during Wales's South American tour in 1962. He collided heavily with striker Vavà. Kelsey complained of back pains and specialists discovered a spinal injury. Kelsey was a one-club man and had been at Highbury for 13 years. He was rewarded by being made manager of the Arsenal club shop, where he worked until his retirement in 1989.

Dave Bowen died in 1995, aged 67. A year after the World Cup he returned to Northampton Town as player-manager – at 32 he was the league's youngest manager – and in an incredible six-year period he led them from Division Four to Division One, a feat matched only by Graham Taylor at Watford and John Toshack at Swansea City. In 1964 he replaced Jimmy Murphy as Wales manager on a part-time basis. Results during the Bowen era were hardly impressive and in 1966, 1967, 1969 and 1972, Wales failed to win a single international. Bowen was offered the job full-time in 1974 but he turned it down. "I would love to have done the job, but the contract and wages were not acceptable for the task involved," said Bowen, who was then general manager at Northampton. The Welsh FA appointed Mike Smith instead. Bowen later became secretary and then a director at Northampton before retiring from football in 1989 to start a bookmaking business.

'Golden Boy' Ivor Allchurch died in 1997, aged 67. After receiving rave reports from the World Cup (Santiago Bernabeu, the man who made Real Madrid one of the most famous clubs in the world, described Allchurch as the best inside-forward of the 1958 series), Allchurch finally left Swansea and joined a Division One side, Newcastle United. It was not a good move. Newcastle were struggling at the time and were relegated in 1962, although in his 143 appearances for the Magpies he scored 46 goals. Allchurch then joined Cardiff City and played in their first ever Cup Winners Cup adventure. His last game for Wales was against Chile in 1966 and his 68 appearances was a record for 20 years until it was broken by Joey Jones.

Roy Vernon, who made a solitary World Cup appearance against Sweden, died in 1993, aged 56. Vernon had been ill for some time, with arthritis of the hip and spine. He joined Everton from Blackburn in 1960. In 1963 the Merseysiders were league champions. Vernon, the captain, scored a hat-trick in the decisive match, a 4–1 win over Fulham. He was Everton's top scorer for four seasons and he formed a lethal partnership with Alex Young. He joined Stoke City in 1965 and moved to South Africa with Cape Town in 1970. After retiring from football, he ran an antiques business.

Colin Baker was the only other player to have featured in the finals, appearing against Mexico. Baker, now 63, lives in his native Cardiff, in a semi-detached house in the Rhiwbina area. He started and finished his professional career with his hometown club. He was part of the City team which won promotion to Division One in 1960 and he retired from the game five years later. In 1967, along with Derek Tapscott, he was invited by City chairman Fred Dewey to run the club's fundraising department. Baker accepted and stayed until 1973. "I'd had enough by then," says Baker. "I wanted a change from football." He then became a clerk at Cardiff Magistrates Court and in February 1998 he took early retirement.

Ken Jones and Ken Leek were the two members of 'the Big Five' who failed to get a kick in the 1958 competition. Jones lives in a ground-floor flat in his beloved Cwmbach, near Aberdare. He left Cardiff City for Scunthorpe United where he was hugely popular with supporters. He quit Scunthorpe after team-mate Ronnie Howells was exposed as one of 10 players – Tony Kay, Peter Swan and 'Bronco' Lane were among the others – who had accepted bribes to throw matches. "I was approached by Jimmy Gauld (Gauld, an ex-footballer, was the Mr Fix-It behind the scandal). Someone told me he wanted to see me about business. I thought he wanted to sign me for another club, so I met him in a transport café in Mansfield," says Jones. "He told me what was on offer. I said 'No way' and I was out of there. They wanted me because I was the goalkeeper. They could bribe defenders, but if I played a blinder in goal I could ruin their scam. After me they must have gone to Ronnie."

Jones later played for Barnsley, Charlton Athletic, Exeter City and Yeovil Town. He never played for Wales. "I remember one time Jack (Kelsey) was injured. They picked Tony Millington, who was the reserve at West Brom, ahead of me. I knew that was the end for me," he explains. "Still, I went to the World Cup. Not many players can say that, can they?" For 10 years he worked as a storeman for Yeovil-based engineers Westland before returning home to Cwmbach. "I ran a couple of pubs," he says. "One in Cwmbach and one in Aberdare. Then I had TB. I was in hospital for five months." Jones recovered and became a sports consultant for a sports centre in

Aberdare. After four years he lost his job due to cutbacks. "I decided to retire after that."

Ken Leek is 63. He is retired and lives in Northampton. Leek stayed at Leicester until 1961. He left following a row with manager Matt Gillies. "He was unhappy I was playing for Wales. When the results were OK he let me play for Wales. When results were going badly he wanted me to play in the league." When Gillies dropped him for the 1961 FA Cup Final, against Tottenham, Leek was incensed. He played in the third, fourth, fifth, sixth rounds, the quarter-final and the semi-final. But not the final. He joined Newcastle in 1961 and then Birmingham City, Northampton Town, Bradford City, Rhyl, Merthyr Tydfil and Ton Pentre. He worked in packaging at the Ford parts factory in Daventry for 22 years before retiring at 60 in 1995. "I'm not rich but I've got a nice detached house," he says.

Vic Crowe and Trevor Edwards were the remaining squad players who, like Leek and Ken Jones, did not make an appearance in Sweden. Crowe had to wait until November 1958 for his international debut, against England at Villa Park, the ground he played on week-in week-out. He was part of the Aston Villa team which won promotion to Division One in 1960 and he also captained the Midlands outfit to League Cup success a year later. He joined Peterborough and then moved into management with Atlanta Chiefs in the North American League, where he was assistant to another ex-Welsh international, Phil Woosnam. When Villa sacked manager Tommy Docherty in 1970, Crowe was an obvious candidate to take over. Despite guiding them to another League Cup final, as well as promotion to Division Two, Crowe, now 66, was sacked in 1974 after poor results. He returned to the North American League as manager of Portland Timbers before returning to Britain to work in an advisory capacity for Bilston Town.

Trevor Edwards is 61 and now lives in Australia, his home for the last 34 years. He was at Charlton until 1960 before signing for Cardiff City where he stayed until 1964. Then he moved 'Down Under' where he became captain and coach of Sydney club Hakoah. He then joined another Aussie club, Marconi, and led them to the Australian championship. Edwards even played for Australia but that ended when a new naturalisation rule was introduced. Edwards, who refused to give up his British passport, was forced to abandon a second international career.

THE 1958 WORLD CUP

GROUP ONE

NORTHERN IRELAND 1 CZECHOSLOVAKIA 0 (H-T 1-0)

Örjans Vall, Halmstad
June 8
Northern Ireland: Gregg; Keith; McMichael; Blanchflower; Cunningham; Peacock; Bingham; Cush; Dougan; McIlroy; McParland.
Czechoslovakia: Dolejsi; Mraz; Novák, Pluskal; Cadek; Masopust; Hovorka; Dvorak; Borovicka; Hertl; Kraus.
Goals: Cush
Attendance: 10,647
Referee: Eric Seipelt (Austria)

WEST GERMANY 3 ARGENTINA 1 (H-T 2-1)

Malmö Stadium, Malmö
June 8
West Germany: Herkenrath; Stollenwerk; Juskowiak; Eckel; Erhardt; Szymaniak; Rahn; Walter; Seeler; Schmidt; Schäfer.
Argentina: Carrizo; Lombardo; Vairo; Rossi; Dellacha; Varacka; Corbatta; Prado; Menendez; Rojas; Cruz.
Goals: Corbatta, Rahn, Seeler, Rahn
Attendance: 31,156
Referee: Reg Leafe (England)

ARGENTINA 3 NORTHERN IRELAND 1 (1-1)

Örjans Vall, Halmstad
June 11
Argentina: Carrizo; Lombardo; Vairo; Rossi; Dellacha; Varacka;
Corbatta; Avio; Menendez; Labruna; Boggio.
Northern Ireland: Gregg; Keith; McMichael; Blanchflower;
Cunningham; Peacock; Bingham; Cush; Coyle; McIlroy;
McParland.
Goals: McParland, Corbatta (pen), Menendez, Avio
Attendance: 14,174
Referee: Arthur Ellis (England)

CZECHOSLOVAKIA 2 WEST GERMANY 2 (H-T 2-0)

Olympia Stadium, Halsingborg
June 11
Czechoslovakia: Dolejsi; Mraz; Novák; Pluskal; Popluhár;
Masopust; Hovorka; Dvorak; Molnar; Feureisl; Zikan.
West Germany: Herkenrath; Stollenwerk; Juskowiak; Schnellinger;
Erhardt; Szymaniak; Rahn; Seeler; Schäfer; Klodt.
Goals: Dvorak (pen), Zikan, Schäfer, Rahn
Attendance: 25,000
Referee: Arthur Ellis (England)

NORTHERN IRELAND 2 WEST GERMANY 2 (H-T 1-1)

Malmö Stadium, Malmö
June 15
Northern Ireland: Gregg; Keith; McMichael; Blanchflower;
Cunningham; Peacock; Bingham; Cush; Casey; McIlroy;
McParland.
West Germany: Herkenrath; Stollenwerk; Juskowiak; Eckel;
Erhardt; Szymaniak; Rahn; Walter; Seeler; Schäfer; Klodt.
Goals: McParland, Rahn, McParland, Seeler
Attendance: 21,990
Referee: Joaquim Campos (Portugal)

CZECHOSLOVAKIA 6 ARGENTINA 1 (H-T 3-0)

Olympia Stadium, Halsingborg
June 15
Czechoslovakia: Dolejsi; Mraz; Novák; Dvorak; Popluhár;
Masopust; Hovorka; Borovicka; Molnar; Feureisl; Zikan.
Argentina: Carrizo; Lombardo; Vairo; Rossi; Dellacha; Varacka;
Corbatta; Avio; Menendez; Labruna; Cruz.
Goals: Dvorak, Zikan, Zikan, Corbatta (pen), Feureisl; Hovorka,
Hovorka
Attendance: 16,418
Referee: Arthur Ellis (England)

GROUP ONE FINAL TABLE

	P	W	L	D	Pts
West Germany	3	1	0	2	4
Northern Ireland	3	1	1	1	3
Czechoslovakia	3	1	1	1	3
Argentina	3	1	2	0	2

PLAY-OFF
NORTHERN IRELAND 2 CZECHOSLOVAKIA 1 (a.e.t.) (H-T 1-1; 90 mins 1-1)

Malmö Stadium, Malmö
June 17
Northern Ireland: Uprichard; Keith; McMichael; Blanchflower;
Cunningham; Peacock; Bingham; Cush; Scott; McIlroy; McParland.
Czechoslovakia: Dolejsi; Mraz; Novák; Bubernik; Popluhár;
Masopust; Dvorak; Borovicka; Feureisl; Molnar; Zikan.
Goals: McParland, Zikan, McParland
Attendance: 6,196
Referee: Maurice Guigue (France)

GROUP TWO

SCOTLAND 1 YUGOSLAVIA 1 (H-T 0-1)

Arosvallen, Västeras
June 8
Scotland: Younger; Caldow; Hewie; Turnbull; Evans; Cowie;
Leggat; Murray; Mudie; Collins; Imlach.
Yugoslavia: Beara; Sijakovic; Crnkovic; Krstic; Zebec; Boskov;
Petakovic; Veselinovic; Milutinovic; Sekularac; Rajkov.
Goals: Petakovic, Murray
Attendance: 9,591
Referee: Paul Wyssling (Switzerland)

FRANCE 7 PARAGUAY 3 (H-T 2-2)

Idrottsparken, Norrköping
June 8
France: Remetter; Kaelbel; Lerond; Penverne; Jonquet; Marcel;
Wisnieski; Fontaine; Kopa; Piantoni; Vincent.
Paraguay: Mageregger; Arevalo; Miranda; Achucaro; Lezcano;
Villalba; Aguero; Parodi; Romero; Re; Amarilla.
Goals: Amarilla, Fontaine, Fontaine, Amarilla (pen), Romero,
Piantoni, Wisnieski, Fontaine, Kopa, Vincent
Attendance: 16,518
Referee: Juan Gardeazabal Garay (Spain)

PARAGUAY 3 SCOTLAND 2 (H-T 2-1)

Idrottsparken, Norrköping
June 11
Paraguay: Aguilar; Arevalo; Echague; Achucaro; Lezcano;
Villalba; Aguero; Parodi; Romero; Re; Amarilla.
Scotland: Younger; Parker; Caldow; Turnbull; Evans; Cowie;
Leggat; Collins; Mudie; Robertson; Fernie.
Goals: Aguero, Mudie, Re, Parodi, Collins
Attendance: 11,665
Referee: Vincenzo Orlandini (Italy)

YUGOSLAVIA 3 FRANCE 2 (H-T 1-1)

Arosvallen, Västeras
June 11
Yugoslavia: Beara; Tomic; Crnkovic; Krstic; Zebec; Boskov;
Petakovic; Veselinovic; Milutinovic; Sekularac; Rajkov.
France: Remetter; Kaelbel; March; Penverne; Jonquet; Lerond;
Wisnieski; Fontaine; Kopa; Piantoni; Vincent.
Goals: Fontaine, Petakovic, Veselinovic, Fontaine, Veselinovic
Attendance: 12,217
Referee: Mervyn Griffiths (Wales)

FRANCE 2 SCOTLAND 1 (H-T 2-0)

Eyravallen, Örebro
June 15
France: Abbès; Kaelbel; Lerond; Penverne; Jonquet; Marcel;
Wisnieski; Fontaine; Kopa; Piantoni; Vincent.
Scotland: Brown; Caldow; Hewie; Turnbull; Evans; Mackay;
Collins; Murray; Mudie; Baird; Imlach.
Goals: Kopa, Fontaine, Baird
Attendance: 13,554
Referee: Juan Brozzi (Argentina)

PARAGUAY 3 YUGOSLAVIA 3 (H-T 1-2)

Tunavallen, Eskilstuna
June 15
Paraguay: Aguilar; Arevalo; Echague; Villalba; Lezcano;
Achucaro; Aguero; Parodi; Romero; Re; Amarilla.
Yugoslavia: Beara; Tomic; Crnkovic; Krstic; Zebec; Boskov;
Petakovic; Veselinovic; Ognjanovic; Sekularac; Rajkov.
Goals: Ognjanovic, Parodi, Veselinovic, Aguero, Rajkov, Romero
Attendance: 13,103
Referee: Martin Macko (Czechoslovakia)

GROUP TWO FINAL TABLE

	P	W	L	D	Pts
France	3	2	1	0	4
Yugoslavia	3	1	0	2	4
Paraguay	3	1	1	1	3
Scotland	3	0	2	1	1

GROUP THREE

SWEDEN 3 MEXICO 0 (H-T 1-0)

Rasunda Stadium, Stockholm
June 8
Sweden: Svensson; Bergmark; Axbom; Liedholm; Gustavsson;
Parling; Hamrin; Mellberg; Simonsson; Gren; Skoglund.
Mexico: Carbajal; Del Muro; Villegas; Portugal; Romo; Flores;
Hernández; Reyes; Calderon; Gutiérrez; Sesma.
Goals: Simonsson, Simonsson, Liedholm (pen)
Attendance: 34,107
Referee: Nikolai Latychev (USSR)

HUNGARY 1 WALES 1 (H-T 1-1)

Jernallen, Sandviken
June 8
Hungary: Grosics; Mátrai; Sárosi; Bozsik; Sipos; Berendi; Sándor;
Hidegkuti; Tichy; Bundszák; Fenyvesi.
Wales: Kelsey; Williams; Hopkins; Sullivan, M.Charles; Bowen;
Webster; Medwin; J.Charles; Allchurch; Jones.
Goals: Bozsik, J.Charles
Attendance: 15,343
Referee: José Maria Codesal (Uruguay)

MEXICO 1 WALES 1 (H-T 0-1)

Rasunda Stadium, Stockholm
June 11
Mexico: Carbajal; Del Muro; Gutiérrez; Cardenas; Romo; Flores;
Belmonte; Reyes; Blanco; González; Sesma.
Wales: Kelsey; Williams; Hopkins; Baker; M.Charles; Bowen;
Webster; Medwin; J.Charles; Allchurch; Jones.
Goals: Allchurch, Belmonte
Attendance: 15,150
Referee: Leo Lemesic (Yugoslavia)

SWEDEN 2 HUNGARY 1 (H-T 1-0)

Rasunda Stadium, Stockholm
June 15
Sweden: Svensson; Bergmark; Axborn; Liedholm; Gustavsson;
Parling; Hamrin; Mellberg; Simonsson; Skoglund.
Hungary: Grosics; Mátrai; Sárosi; Szojka; Sipos; Berendi; Sándor;
Tichy; Bozsik; Bundzsák, Fenyvesi.
Goals: Hamrin, Hamrin, Tichy
Attendance: 38,850
Referee: Jack Mowatt (Scotland)

SWEDEN 0 WALES 0 (H-T 0-0)

Rasunda Stadium, Stockholm
June 15
Sweden: Svensson; Bergmark; Axbom; Börjesson; Gustavsson;
Parling; Berndtsson; Selmonsson; Källgren; Löfgren; Skoglund.
Wales: Kelsey; Williams; Hopkins; Sullivan; M.Charles, Bowen;
Vernon; Hewitt; J.Charles; Allchurch; Jones.
Attendance: 29,800
Referee: Lucien Van Nuffel (Belgium)

HUNGARY 4 MEXICO 0 (H-T 1-0)

Jernvallen, Sandviken
June 15
Hungary: Ilku; Mátrai; Sárosi; Szojka; Sipos; Kotász; Budai;
Bencsics; Bozsik; Tichy; Sándor.
Mexico: Carbajal; Del Muro; Gutiérrez; Cardenas; Sepúlveda;
Flores; Belmonte; Reyes; Blanco; González; Sesma.
Goals: Tichy, Tichy, Sándor, González (og)
Referee: A. Eriksson (Finland)
Attendance: 13,310

GROUP THREE FINAL TABLE

	P	W	L	D	Pts
Sweden	3	2	0	1	5
Hungary	3	1	1	1	3
Wales	3	0	0	3	3
Mexico	3	0	2	1	1

PLAY-OFF

WALES 2 HUNGARY 1 (H-T 0-1)

Rasunda Stadium, Stockholm
June 17
Wales: Kelsey; Williams; Hopkins; Sullivan; M.Charles; Bowen;
Medwin; Hewitt; J.Charles; Allchurch; Jones.
Hungary: Grosics; Mátrai; Sárosi; Bozsik; Sipos; Kotász; Budai;
Bencsics; Tichy; Bundzsák; Fenyvesi.
Goals: Tichy, Allchurch, Medwin
Attendance: 2,832
Referee: Nikolai Latychev (USSR)

GROUP FOUR

BRAZIL 3 AUSTRIA 0 (H-T 1-0)

Rimnersvallen, Uddevalla
June 8
Brazil: Gilmar; De Sordi N. Santos; Dino; Bellini; Orlando; Joel;
Didi; Altafini; Dida; Zagallo.
Austria: Szanwald; Halla; Swoboda; Hanappi; Happel; Koller;
Horak; Senekowitsch; Buzek; Körner; Schleger.
Goals: Altafini, N.Santos, Altafini
Referee: Maurice Guigue (France)

ENGLAND 2 SOVIET UNION 2 (H-T 0-1)

Nya Ullevi Stadium, Gothenburg
June 8
England: McDonald; Howe; Banks; Clamp; Wright; Slater;
Douglas; Robson; Kevan; Haynes; Finney.
Soviet Union: Yashin, Kesarev, Kuzetsov, Voinov, Krijevski,
Tsarev, A.Ivanov, V.Ivanov, Simonian, Salnikov, Ilyin.
Goals: Simonian, A.Ivanov, Kevan, Finney (pen)
Attendance: 49,348
Referee: Istvan Zsolt (Hungary)

BRAZIL 0 ENGLAND 0 (H-T 0-0)

Nya Ullevi Stadium, Gothenburg
June 11
Brazil: Gilmar; De Sordi; N.Santos; Dino; Bellini; Orlando; Joel;
Didi; Altafini; Vavà; Zagallo.
England: McDonald; Howe; Banks; Clamp; Wright; Slater;
Douglas; Robson; Kevan; Haynes; A'Court.
Attendance: 40,895
Referee: Albert Dusch (West Germany)

SOVIET UNION 2 AUSTRIA 0 (H-T 1-0)

Ryavallen, Boras
June 11
Soviet Union: Yashin; Kesarev; Kuznetsov; Voinov; Krijevski;
Tsarev; A.Ivanov; V.Ivanov; Simonian; Salnikov; Ilyin.
Austria: Schmied; E.Kozlicek; Swoboda; Hanappi; Stotz; Koller;
Horak; P. Kozlicek; Buzek; Körner; Senekowitsch.
Goals: Ilyin, V.Ivanov
Attendance: 21,239
Referee: Carl Jorgensen (Denmark)

BRAZIL 2 SOVIET UNION 0 (H-T 1-0)

Nya Ullevi Stadium, Gothenburg
June 15
Brazil: Gilmar; De Sordi; N.Santos; Zito; Bellini; Orlando;
Garrincha; Didi; Vavà; Pelé; Zagallo
Soviet Union: Yashin; Kesarev; Kuznetsov; Voinov; Krijevski;
Tsarev; A.Ivanov; V.Ivanov; Simonian; Netto; Ilyin.
Goals: Vavà, Vavà
Attendance: 50,928
Referee: Maurice Guigue (France)

AUSTRIA 2 ENGLAND 2 (H-T 1-0)

Ryavallen, Boras
June 15
Austria: Szanwald; Kollmann; Swoboda; Hanappi; Happel;
Koller; E. Kozlicek; P. Kozlicek; Buzek; Körner; Senekowitsch.
England: McDonald; Howe; Banks; Clamp; Wright; Slater;
Douglas; Robson; Kevan; Haynes; A'Court.
Goals: Koller, Haynes, Körner, Kevan
Attendance: 16,800
Referee: A. Asmussen (Denmark)

GROUP FOUR FINAL TABLE

	P	W	L	D	Pts
Brazil	3	2	0	1	5
England	3	0	0	3	3
Soviet Union	3	1	1	1	3
Austria	3	0	2	1	1

PLAY-OFF

SOVIET UNION 1 ENGLAND 0 (H-T 0-0)

Nya Ullevi Stadium, Gothenburg
June 17
Soviet Union: Yashin; Kesarev; Kuznetsov; Voinov; Krijevski;
Tsarev; Apoukhtin; V.Ivanov; Simonian; Falin; Ilyin.
England: McDonald; Howe; Banks; Clayton; Wright; Slater;
Brabrook; Broadbent; Kevan; Haynes; A'Court.
Goals: Ilyin
Attendance: 23,182
Referee: Albert Dusch (West Germany)

THE QUARTER-FINALS

BRAZIL 1 WALES 0 (H-T 0-0)

Nya Ullevi Stadium, Gothenburg
June 19
Brazil: Gilmar; De Sordi; N.Santos; Zito; Bellini; Orlando;
Garrincha; Didi; Altafini; Pelé; Zagallo.
Wales: Kelsey; Williams; Hopkins; Sullivan; M.Charles; Bowen;
Medwin; Hewitt; Webster; Allchurch; Jones.
Goals: Pelé
Attendance: 25,923
Referee: Erich Seipelt (Austria)

FRANCE 4 NORTHERN IRELAND 0 (H-T 1-0)

Idrottsparken, Norrköping
June 19
France: Abbès; Kaelbel; Lerond; Penverne; Jonquet; Marcel;
Wisnieski; Fontaine; Kopa; Piantoni; Vincent.
Northern Ireland: Gregg; Keith; McMichael; Blanchflower;
Cunningham; Cush; Bingham; Casey; Scott; McIlroy; McParland.
Goals: Wisnieski, Fontaine, Fontaine, Piantoni
Attendance: 11,800
Referee: Juan Gardeazabal Garay (Spain)

SWEDEN 2 SOVIET UNION 0 (H-T 0-0)

Rasunda Stadium, Stockholm
June 19
Sweden: Svensson; Bergmark; Axbom; Börjesson; Gustavsson;
Parling; Hamrin; Gren; Simonsson; Liedholm; Skoglund.
Soviet Union: Yashin; Kesarev; Kuznetsov; Voinov; Krijevski;
Tsarev; A.Ivanov; V.Ivanov; Simonian; Salnikov; Ilyin.
Goals: Hamrin, Simonsson
Referee: Reg Leafe

WEST GERMANY 1 YUGOSLAVIA 0 (H-T 1-0)

Malmö Stadium, Malmö
June 19
West Germany: Herkenrath; Stollenwerk; Juskowiak; Eckel;
Erhardt; Szymaniak; Rahn; Walter; Seeler; Schmidt; Schäfer.
Yugoslavia: Krivokuca; Sijakovic; Crnkovic; Krstic; Zebec;
Boskov; Petakovic; Ognjanovic; Milutinovic; Veselinovic; Rajkov.
Goals: Rahn
Attendance: 20,000
Referee: Paul Wyssling (Switzerland)

THE SEMI-FINALS

BRAZIL 5 FRANCE 2 (H-T 2-1)

Rasunda Stadium, Stockholm
June 24
Brazil: Gilmar; De Sordi; N.Santos; Zito; Bellini; Orlando;
Garrincha; Didi; Vavà; Pelé; Zagallo.
France: Abbès; Kaelbel; Lerond; Penverne; Jonquet; Marcel;
Wisnieski; Fontaine; Kopa; Piantoni; Vincent.
Goals: Vavà, Fontaine, Didi, Pelé, Pelé, Pelé, Piantoni
Attendance: 27,100
Referee: Mervyn Griffiths (Wales)

SWEDEN 3 WEST GERMANY 1 (H-T 1-1)

Nya Ullevi Stadium, Gothenburg
June 24
Sweden: Svensson; Bergmark; Axbom; Börjesson; Gustavsson;
Parling; Hamrin; Gren; Simonsson; Liedholm; Skoglund.
West Germany: Herkenrath; Stollenwerk; Juskowiak; Eckel;
Erhardt; Szymaniak; Rahn; Walter; Seeler; Schäfer; Cieslarczyk.
Goals: Schäfer, Skoglund, Gren, Hamrin
Attendance: 49,471
Referee: Istvan Zsolt (Hungary)

THIRD PLACE PLAY-OFF

FRANCE 6 WEST GERMANY 3 (H-T 3-1)

Nya Ullevi Stadium, Gothenburg
June 28
France: Abbés; Kaelbel; Lerond; Penverne; Lafont; Marcel;
Wisnieski; Douis; Kopa; Fontaine; Vincent.
West Germany: Kwiatkowski; Stollenwerk; Erhardt; Schnellinger;
Wewers; Szymaniak; Rahn; Sturm; Kelbassa; Schäfer; Cieslarczyk.
Goals: Fontaine, Cieslarczyk, Kopa (pen), Fontaine, Douis, Rahn,
Fontaine, Schäfer, Fontaine.
Attendance: 32,482
Referee: Juan Brozzi (Argentina)

THE FINAL

BRAZIL 5 SWEDEN 2 (H-T 2-1)

Rasunda Stadium, Stockholm
June 29
Brazil: Gilmar; D.Santos; N.Santos; Zito; Bellini; Orlando;
Garrincha; Didi; Vavà; Pelé; Zagallo.
Sweden: Svensson: Bergmark; Axbom; Börjesson; Gustavsson;
Parling; Hamrin; Gren; Simonsson; Liedholm; Skoglund.
Goals: Liedholm, Vavà, Vavà, Pelé, Zagallo, Simonsson, Pelé
Attendance: 49,737
Referee: Maurice Guigue (France)